HARRY
HOUDINI'S

Paper
Magic

HARRY HOUDINI'S

Paper Magic

The Whole Art of Paper Tricks, Including Folding, Tearing & Puzzles

Dover Publications, Inc.
Mineola, New York

Bibliographical Note

This Dover edition, first published in 2017, is an unabridged republication of the work originally published by E. P. Dutton & Company, New York, in 1922, under the title *Houdini's Paper Magic*. The original full-color frontispiece has been reproduced here on the inside front cover.

International Standard Book Number:

ISBN-13: 978-0-486-81477-3
ISBN-10: 0-486-81477-7

Manufactured in the United States by LSC Communications
81477701   2017
www.doverpublications.com

I dedicate this book to the memory of
my dear old friend and private secretary

John William Sargent

to whom I am indebted for many a
cheerful hour of interesting conversation, and who always endeavored to
make me look upon life as a pleasant
voyage instead of a continual struggle
for existence and a survival of the fittest.

—HOUDINI.

CONTENTS

PART ONE

PAPER TRICKS

PAGE

The Travelling Paper Balls.......................... 3

Ring and Program.................................... 8

The Cigarette-Paper Tear........................... 13

The Torn Paper Ribbon.............................. 20

The Restored Calendar.............................. 24

The Selective Touch................................ 29

The Dancing Sailor................................. 33

The Spirit Communication........................... 37

The Knife and Paper Sleight........................ 40

The Chameleon Confetti............................. 43

Production of Confetti............................. 49

Another Confetti Change............................ 51

Watered Confetti................................... 54

The Floating Ball.................................. 57

The Japanese Butterflies........................... 61

The Shaving Stick.................................. 65

The Paper Flags.................................... 69

The Pig and the Ring............................... 71

Coffee, Milk and Sugar............................. 79

The Ballot or Pellet Test.......................... 83

Paper Clippings and Water.......................... 93

Werner's Bill Tearing Trick........................ 99

An Effective Finish................................ 110

CONTENTS

PART TWO

PAPER FOLDING

PAGE

The Japanese Bird.................................... 117

The Bullfrog.. 122

Puzzle Box for Sweets............................... 127

Trouble Wit... 130

The Chapeau... 133

Japanese Paper Purse................................ 136

Japanese Hexagon Puzzle Box......................... 139

PART THREE

PAPER TEARING

Trewey's Paper Rings................................ 143

Jacob's Ladder...................................... 147

The Trellis... 150

The Fir Tree.. 152

The Dancing Skeletons............................... 154

Grandma's String of Dolls........................... 159

The Dancing Girls................................... 161

Paper Pictures...................................... 163

Circular Designs.................................... 167

The Five-Pointed Star............................... 176

Tearing the Pack.................................... 178

PART FOUR

PAPER PUZZLES

Paper Puzzles....................................... 183

The Symmetrical Square Puzzle....................... 188

The Stairs.. 189

The Hexagon Puzzle 190

CONTENTS

PAGE

THE OCTAGON PUZZLE.................................... 191

THE HOUSE AND ELL PUZZLE........................... 192

THE CROSS AND CRESCENT.............................. 193

THE LATIN CROSS...................................... 194

THE SHORT DOZEN...................................... 196

THE RIGHT-ANGLE TRIANGLE........................... 197

THE GREEK CROSS PUZZLE.............................. 198

THE SQUARE DEAL PUZZLE.............................. 199

TO PASS THROUGH A CARD.............................. 200

THE LIBERTY BELL..................................... 202

THE CROSS CUT PUZZLE................................ 204

THE THREE CROSSES.................................... 205

PART ONE
PAPER TRICKS

HOUDINI'S
PAPER MAGIC

THE TRAVELLING PAPER BALLS

THE following is a good impromptu combination that can be done anywhere, no preparation being necessary.

Roll up three paper pellets about the size of a pea and throw them on a table or chair seat where all can see them. Then showing the right hand empty, pick up a pellet with the thumb and finger of the left and place it in the right, saying, "one," and immediately closing the hand. Repeat with the second, saying, "two." Pick up the third and say: "This one we will send on its travels." Throw it under some piece of furniture or out of the window, and immediately opening the right hand, throw the three pellets on the chair.

Continue, "Didn't you catch it? I'll do it

again." Proceed as before, but after counting "one," and closing the right hand, stop, as if someone had questioned the move, open the right hand and show that there is only one pellet there, close the hand and finish as before.

Now say, "Perhaps some of you can't see how it is done even now, probably because the balls are too small. Let's try it with larger ones." Take a page of a newspaper and tear it into quarters, rolling each piece into a ball about the size of a golf-ball and placing them on the floor in a quadrangle about eighteen inches apart. Then borrow two hats and place over the two balls farthest from you, and put the other two balls one on top of each hat. Pick the ball from the top of the left hand hat with the left hand and transfer it to the right, and make a motion as if tossing it in the air, showing the right hand empty. Then point with that hand as if following the ball as it invisibly falls toward the left-hand hat. On lifting the hat, two balls will be found under it. Cover these again and repeat the process with the other ball. Raise the hat and show

three balls. Cover once more and command
the ball under the right hand hat to join the
others under the left without your assistance.
When the right hand hat is lifted the ball has
vanished and the four will be found under the
left.

EXPLANATION.—When rolling the small pellets make four instead of three and hold the
fourth one concealed between the points of the
first and second fingers of the left hand. When
you put the first ball in the right hand, drop
the concealed one with it and carelessly show
the left hand empty. Pick up the second one
openly and place it in the right hand, opening
the hand only enough to slip the ball in, not
enough to show the others. Take up the third
ball and pretend to throw it away, but really
roll it into the concealed position at the tips of
the fingers and immediately throw down the
three from the right hand.

The second time you put only one ball in
the right hand, still holding the extra ball hidden. Display the single ball in the right hand,
as described above. Close the hand and pick

up the second pellet, and as you place it in the right hand leave the hidden ball also. This time you really throw away the third ball, produce the three and show both hands empty.

The passing of the large ball is an entirely different trick, but you should make it appear that it is only an enlargement of the above.

Roll up the four balls and place them on the floor as in the above description. Hold the two hats by the rims with the thumbs on top and the fingers underneath. Remark that it does not make any difference which ones you cover, at the same time holding the hats first over one pair and then over another, passing quickly from one to the other. At last bring the hat held in the right hand over the ball in the upper corner on that side in such a way that the back of your fingers rest on the ball, and, clipping a fold of this ball between the middle fingers, draw the hand away from the hat with the ball held on the back. At the same instant pass the hat held in the left hand over to the right, so that when the hand comes from beneath the first hat the other is above it, and the right hand immediately seizes this hat by the brim as before, which brings the ball inside. The hat is carried across and dropped on the left hand ball and the hand withdrawn, thus leaving the two balls together. A ball is now placed on top of each hat.

With the left hand pick up the ball from the top of the hat on that side and pretend to pass it into the right, in reality palming it in the left hand by pinching a fold between the thumb and the side of the hand. Make the throwing motion as described and as you stoop down it is a perfectly natural move to place the left hand on the left leg above the knee while reaching with the right to turn over the hat. This will effectually conceal the ball held in that hand. Raise the hat and show the two balls. As soon as the hat is raised it is passed to the left hand and while that hand is covered the ball is brought to the finger tips and held inside as before and the hat dropped over the two balls. Repeat this with the other ball. As they are now all together, the rest of the trick is merely conversation.

THIS was one of the best features of the program given by Guibal when he played at the Eden Musée many years ago. It was not new even at that time; in fact, I had made it a part of my own show in my amateur days; but it is extremely effective if properly handled, and it has always been a surprise to me that it has not come into more general use.

Guibal probably learned the trick from Verbeck, for whom he acted as interpreter during the tour of the latter in England. His clever patter is said to have greatly benefited the Verbeck performance, but later there was a disagreement, and Guibal started for himself, giving practically the same program.

The effect of the trick in question is as follows: A wedding ring is borrowed from a lady in the audience, and a program from another. A volunteer assistant is invited upon the stage, asked to watch every move and see that no deception is practised. The performer then brings a small hammer from his table and asks the volunteer to hammer the ring flat, but stops him in order first to get the consent of the lady. Her answer being "yes," he then says, "Then, madam, the 'yes' that you have just spoken is as irrevocable as your 'yes' when you received the ring."

The volunteer now hammers the ring perfectly flat. Meanwhile the performer has torn a leaf from the program and holds it spread on his open right palm, with his thumb on top. The assistant places the ring on the paper, sliding it under the thumb of the performer, who immediately crushes it up into a rough package and passes it with the same hand to the gentleman, the left hand never having approached the right, and asks him to hold it a moment. Turning to his table, he picks up a stick of sealing-wax and with it makes three quick motions toward the crushed program and then asks him to open it. On doing so, the assistant finds that the program has changed to an envelope, sealed with sealing-wax. Opening this he finds another smaller one, and inside this still another, which contains the ring restored to its original shape.

After the young man acknowledges that he does not see how it has been done, the performer does it all over again. This time the last envelope is opened by the owner of the ring, who finds it fully restored.

EXPLANATION.—The borrowed ring is on the end of the performer's wand, a dummy ring being held on the opposite end covered by the hand. By changing the wand from hand to hand the rings are "switched" and the dummy is given to the volunteer to hold. When going to the table for the hammer, the borrowed ring is left there, and while the dummy is being flattened, the stage assistant carries off the original while taking away some other apparatus. The assistant places this ring inside a set of three envelopes made from a program exactly like the borrowed one, and a little later it is brought on and left behind some object on the table.

During this time the volunteer has flattened

the ring and the performer has spread the leaf of the program on his palm, as above, but at the same time he has taken a duplicate set of envelopes with a duplicate dummy ring in the inner one from beneath his vest and holds it underneath the leaf. This is easily done, as the package is small and is held in place by the thumb. When the leaf is crushed up, the two packages look like one, and when they have been crushed quite small, the envelopes are brought to the top and passed to the volunteer, the other package being retained in the hand. This sounds rather difficult, but a little practice will make the move absolutely invisible.

The performer now turns to his table to get the sealing-wax and gets rid of the palmed package, and the trick proceeds as described above.

For the repetition, while the volunteer is flattening the ring, the performer goes to the table and gets another leaf of the program, and at the same time gets possession of the other set of envelopes, which contains the borrowed ring, and the trick is finished as given above.

Guibal used to finish by gathering up the torn envelopes after the lady had opened the last one and found her ring, and rolling them into a ball, passing them to the lady who had loaned him the program. Upon opening them she found her original program none the worse except for a few wrinkles. This substitution was by the same method used earlier in the trick.

STANDING very high in the aristocracy—one might even say the royalty—of pocket tricks, is our old friend the cigarette trick. Many of the cleverest magicians of our time have held this little illusion in high esteem, and, while the general manipulation is practically the same in all cases, each of the "big fellows" has used some variation reflecting his own individuality.

The bare bones of the trick may be summed up as follows: With the hands shown to be quite empty, a cigarette paper is torn into bits, which are rolled into a ball or pellet. This, being immediately opened, is shown to have been restored to its original form, the pieces seemingly having been magically rejoined. Usually the trick is repeated to "show how it is done," but the repetition only serves to deepen the mystery.

First, I will explain the trick as presented by our late beloved dean, Harry Kellar, who gave me permission to do so.

Kellar folded a duplicate paper into a small packet and stuck it on the left thumb-nail with magician's wax. By holding the hands near the body, palms outward, this was not visible even when he was surrounded by spectators. Holding the other paper in his right hand, he brought the hands together, slowly tore the paper into bits and rolled it into a small packet. Then he switched the packets, leaving the pieces attached to the thumb-nail, and, continuing the slow motions, opened the packet and displayed the apparently restored paper. This he allowed to flutter to the floor, showing the hands empty as at the beginning.

At the first opportunity he shifted the pieces from the nail to the inside of the hand and got rid of them.

Of course he used this only as an impromptu pocket trick and the mystery of the restoration was greatly enhanced by the slow and deliberate manner in which it was presented.

When his audience was all in front, the hands could be held well away from the body without fear of the hidden packet being seen.

Another method is that used by a friend of mine, a society entertainer in New York City, who has supplied me with the following minutely detailed summary of the trick as performed by himself.

First, fold a cigarette paper lengthwise in accordion plaits one-fourth of an inch wide, then fold over and over (not accordion fashion) in the opposite direction in folds of the same size, which makes a package one-fourth of an inch square. I usually have a number of papers thus folded in my pocket, so that I am always prepared for the trick.

Hold this package concealed between the tips of the first and second fingers of the left hand and pick up the "book" of cigarette papers with the same hand, tear out a single paper and hold it between the left thumb and finger while you lay the book aside with the right hand. While doing this, roll the square package to the ball of the left forefinger, which brings it behind the open paper and between the balls of the finger and thumb. Press it firmly against the back of the paper and it becomes entirely invisible from all points of view. Both hands are now displayed, back and front, with the fingers widely distended.

Now, roll the square package back to its position between the fingers and proceed to tear the visible paper into *strips,* not bits, and fold them into a package similar to the concealed package. Fold over and over, so that there may be no loose ends and the last fold will bring the two packages together; then turn once more, which will bring the whole paper to the top and the pieces next to the forefinger, and hold both packages, which look like one, between the points of the two forefingers. This shows that there is nothing concealed anywhere about the hands. Then proceed to open up the whole paper and, in smoothing it out, roll the pack of pieces behind it and press against the back as before. The restored paper can now be freely shown, back and front; but, before anyone has time to figure out where the torn pieces have gone, you say: "Now I am going to show you how it is done." At the same time you crush up the restored paper with the fingers of both hands and pretend to put it in your pocket with the left; what you really do, however, is to leave the torn pieces in the pocket and roll the whole paper to the position between the tips of the fingers as it was at the beginning.

Then, say: "Of course you know by this time that I use two pieces of paper." While saying this take two pieces from the "book," one of which you pass to the left hand, thus covering the concealed pack, and the other you crush up into a pellet. Continue the patter by saying: "One of the papers I show you"— displaying the one in the left hand—"and the other I conceal at the roots of my thumb, thus." Suiting the action to the word you place the pellet between the left thumb and the side of the palm.

Remember, you now hold a whole paper between the thumb and finger of the left hand and pressed against the back of this is another whole one, while a third is held at the roots of the left thumb. Now, tear the open piece into strips and roll into a pellet. With the fingers of the right hand you next pretend to exchange the pellet of torn pieces for the whole paper at the roots of the thumb. As a matter of fact, you do not make the exchange, and right here I use a sleight that I have never seen anyone else introduce into the trick. After tearing the paper I take both the torn strips and the concealed pellet into the right hand and, while rolling up the strips, I conceal the torn pieces between the points of the first and second fingers of the *right* hand. After pretending to make the exchange I return the whole piece only to the fingers of the left. By this means I am enabled to show the left hand empty with the exception of the pack held by the thumb, during the supposed exchange.

Pretend to have a little difficulty in opening out the paper. This gives an excuse for dampening the fingers of the right hand on the tongue, in doing which you leave the torn pieces in the mouth. The little struggle with this paper also dislodges the pack held by the thumb and it drops to the floor, as if by acci-

dent, upon which you say: "That was rather
a bad bungle, but let the pieces lie there for the
present." Then smooth out the paper, showing it to be fully restored, hold it between the
finger and thumb, and with a breath blow it
out into your audience and show both hands
absolutely empty.

Finish by saying: "A magician is always supposed to have something up his sleeve and
what I now have in that suspected locality is
a method of getting out of difficulty in case of
an accident. For instance, these pieces
dropped to the floor"—picking up the pellet—
"and it made no difference, as I was showing
you how the trick was done; but if it had hap-
pened during the first showing I could still
have saved the situation by blowing on the
pieces like this,"—blowing on the pellet—
"which has the effect of knitting them together, as you see." Open the pellet and show
it to be intact, allow it to flutter to the floor and
show the hands back and front with fingers
wide apart.

THE TORN PAPER RIBBON

Ching Ling Foo was the first to present this illusion before an American audience. It was an immediate success and since that time it has, in one form or another, graced the program of nearly every magician and amateur of note throughout this country.

I cannot state positively the method used by Ching, but the most practical of the many forms in general use, and by far the easiest to perform, is by means of the thumb fake. This is a sort of thimble shaped and painted to imitate the first joint of the thumb, in which a duplicate of the ribbon, folded in the shape of an accordion about one inch in length, is loaded. These fakes can be purchased at any magic shop.

In presenting the trick the performer slips the loaded fake onto his right thumb, where it is invisible at a very short distance, and steps forward with a tissue paper ribbon about half an inch wide and three feet long held in the same hand. The ribbon is usually red and is shown to be unprepared. He proceeds to tear the ribbon in half, then in quarters, and so on till he holds thirty-two pieces, each a little over an inch in length.

He then squares up the pieces and at the same time secretly takes the fake from his thumb and withdraws the duplicate ribbon, which he slips up in front of the torn pieces between the thumb and finger of the left hand, fanning out the folds, the folds giving it the appearance of the torn pieces. The latter are now pushed into the fake which is returned to the right thumb, while the same thumb and finger get hold of an end of the ribbon and slowly pull it out to its full length, showing it fully restored and both hands empty.

Some performers repeat the trick "to show how it is done." This effect may be obtained by using another thumb fake or by having the duplicate ribbon in a little package pasted to the back of the original, either at one end or in the middle. As they have seen that the other was without preparation the audience will not notice that you keep a part of one ribbon concealed when repeating the trick.

Begin by saying, "Perhaps I did that a little too fast, I'll do it more slowly, so that you may see just how it is done. Of course I use two ribbons. This one is folded in short lengths and I will hold it here at the side of my thumb." (See description of this move in the cigarette trick, page 15.) Then pick up the other paper and tear it as before. After exchanging the torn pieces for the duplicate, say, "I will now exchange these torn pieces for the whole one." Make the exchange openly and draw out the whole ribbon. In conclusion say, "The best way to get rid of these torn pieces is to join them in the same way." At this moment you draw out the duplicate and show that whole also, with the remark, "Now you know how it is done."

In case the thumb fake is used the second time the torn pieces are loaded into it as before, but if the packet is used the pieces are held between the tips of the first and second fingers of the right hand. In moistening the fingers before drawing out the whole ribbon, the pieces are left in the mouth.

There are several other methods of "getting" the duplicate ribbon. One is to have a little pocket in the front of the coat in which the packet is concealed and a thread which is attached to it so arranged that the thumb can be hooked into it and the packet drawn out. Another is to conceal it under the foot and get hold of it when picking up a piece "accidentally" dropped.

THE RESTORED CALENDAR

None of the principles employed in this clever combination are new, but, as the audience only sees the surface of a trick, the effect is none the worse on that account. If this surface is properly camouflaged, the closer one sticks to the time-tried methods the better.

In effect, the performer takes one of the leaves from an advertising calendar, tears off a corner and gives it to one of the audience to hold. Then he tears the remainder of the leaf into strips, which he rolls into a ball, saying: "There's another month gone, how time flies!" Holding the ball at the tips of the fingers of the left hand, he picks up a fan from the table with the right and fans the strips, at the same time working the ball open with the fingers. He then lays the fan on the table and straightens out the paper, showing the leaf restored. He passes it to the spectator who holds the piece torn from the corner, who fits it in place and reports that the fit is perfect.

He then pretends that someone looks suspicious, and, turning to him says: "I see, sir, that you suspect some trickery on my part, but you wrong me, you really do. I assure you that I am as innocent as an unusually young babe. You think that I kept this original sheet and tore up another. Now just to make you regret all the rest of your life that you so wrongfully mistrusted a fellow mortal, I'm going to sacrifice another month of our all too short life by again tearing this into bits." He proceeds exactly as before, returns to his table, picks up the fan and fans his right hand while walking back toward the audience. Then he straightens it out and again has the corner fitted.

Turning to the suspicious spectator he says, "Sir, I shall expect a public apology from you. Otherwise my second will call on you in the morning."

EXPLANATION.—Three calendar leaves are used, which should be about five by six inches in size and all of the same month. Put two of these together and hold up to the light, taking care that the figures lie exactly one over another. If the edges of the paper are not even, trim with scissors so that the two are exactly alike. Then, holding these close together, tear off a corner. If this is carefully done one of the torn corners will fit either of the leaves. Lay one of the corners on your table and throw the other away. Over the torn corner lay a complete calendar, the top leaf of which must be the same as the prepared ones. One of the prepared leaves is rolled up into a ball and concealed under the vest on the right side, and the other treated in the same way and hidden in the bend of the left elbow.

To begin the trick, pick up the calendar and at the same time the torn corner, which is held against the back at the top, with the left hand, and with the right tear off the leaf, slip it under the left thumb, which is on the front, and draw the calendar away. This will leave the leaf in the left hand with the torn corner held against the back. Now tear off a corner of the leaf, being sure that it is the same corner as that torn from the hidden leaves, and make

the tear as near like the original as possible.
Pass the leaf to the right hand, at the same
time shifting the corners, retaining the one
just torn off in the left hand and substituting
the hidden one. While the left hand is behind
the leaf making the change, crush the last torn
corner into a pellet and get rid of it at the
first opportunity by dropping it on the floor.
Give the other corner to a spectator to hold,
and then tear the leaf into strips, roll into a
ball and hold at the tips of the fingers of the
left hand. Then draw up the sleeve, seemingly
to show that the ball does not "go up the
sleeve," but really to get possession of the ball
concealed in the bend of the elbow.

Pretend to pass the ball from the left to the
right hand, but really palm it at the root of the
left thumb and show the prepared one in its
place. Then, as you pick up the fan, drop the
ball on your servante, or, if you use a black art
table, into the pocket. In the absence of both
of these, have the fan lying on top of a couple
of books and drop the ball behind them. Fan
out the leaf as described above and pass it to

the person holding the torn corner. Of course it will be found to fit perfectly.

Now tear the second leaf as described above, turn and go to your table for the fan. With your back to the audience, get the ball from under the vest and hold it up high where all can see it; at the same time slip the torn pieces under the vest on the other side, and finish as already described.

THOSE familiar with the Hindoo Sand Trick will find here a similar effect without the disagreeable feature of the muddy water. Instead of sand, small pieces of tissue paper are used, and the water is eliminated.

A large glass candy-jar, seven or eight inches high, with an opening sufficiently large for the hand to pass freely into it, is passed for examination together with a tray on which are four paper bags, each containing a quantity of paper clippings. These clippings should be about one inch by an inch and a quarter in size, and each bag filled with a different color: red, white, blue, and green. The combined contents of the bags should be sufficient to fill the jar about three-quarters full.

Have the contents of the bags poured into the jar by one of the audience, thoroughly mixed, and the jar passed to someone to hold, the tray being held by another.

Now, ask the audience to name one of the colors. When this has been done, ask the person who is holding the jar to reach in and take out a handful of the selected color. No matter what he says or does, you remark: "No, not that way! Like this." Plunge your hand into the jar and bring out a handful of the desired color and drop it on the tray. If the color was, for example, blue, you can say, "If you had asked for red it would have been just as easy," and while speaking, reach in again and bring out a handful of red, and toss it on the tray with the other.

Continue by saying, "There are still two other colors. Which do you prefer?" Whichever is chosen, produce it in the same way. Place the jar on the tray and start back toward your table. If anyone should ask for the remaining color, produce it at once; if not, pretend that it is asked for, bring out a handful and, holding the hand high, where all can see it, let the paper fall in a shower on the tray.

The only preparation necessary is to make a small packet of each color, enough to make a fair-sized handful when loosened. Squaring up the pieces as you would a pack of cards, put a strip of tissue paper around them and paste the ends together to hold the pieces secure. A packet about three-quarters of an inch thick will suffice. Secrete two of these under the bottom of the vest on the right side and two on the left, or, if you prefer, one on each side and one in a little pocket sewed on each trouser-leg at the back, just where it can be easily reached by the hand.

When the first color is called for, and while asking the holder of the jar to produce it, get hold of the proper package and hold it in the bend of the fingers; then, with the palm of the hand toward the body, so it cannot be seen, when the proper moment arrives, plunge the hand into the jar and under cover of the other pieces work the package in the hand a moment to break the band and loosen the pieces. Next, holding the hand well above the tray, continue to work the fingers and let the clippings fall a few at a time, by which means they are sep-arated and more or less crushed, thus making a bigger show. While doing this with one hand, secure the second packet with the other and produce as above. While this is being placed on the tray get hold of the third packet, and, while asking for another color to be named, get the fourth in the other hand. Then whichever color is called for, you are prepared, and the fourth is ready for the finish.

THE DANCING SAILOR

THIS very effective little drawing-room trick can be mastered in a few minutes and is quite amusing even after the secret is known.

The figure is cut from twelve pieces of cardboard and when complete should stand about ten inches in height. The pieces are the head, the trunk, two upper arms, two lower arms, two legs—hip to knee—two calves, and two feet. All these should be joined together in the proper places, either by threads knotted at back and front or by wires, in such a manner that they will work freely.

The performer, after taking a seat facing the company, attempts ineffectually three or four times to make the figure stand upright between his feet, which should be far enough apart to give it plenty of room. Each time the Jackey collapses and falls to the floor. The performer then says: "Look out, Jack, here comes the bo'sun." The figure does not move. The performer then blows a boatswain's whistle and the figure rises part way up and remains a few seconds, as if listening, and then drops back again. A long blast on the whistle brings the figure up standing. The performer now begins to whistle the "Sailor's Hornpipe" and the Jackey executes a very funny dance, keeping time to the music. When the music ceases it stands for a few seconds and then collapses as before.

The performer now picks up the figure and passes it to the spectators, who fail to find any "deception" about it.

The secret is quite simple. The magician's faithful friend, the black thread, puts life and agility into the jolly little tar. A thin black silk thread passes from leg to leg of the performer at the height of the sailor's head and the figure is attached to this, as shown in Fig. 1. By keeping time to the music with the heels the sailor is made to dance.

The length of the thread may be determined by experiment and it should have a black pin bent into a hook attached to each end. The thread should pass back of the calves of the legs and be fastened to the outer seam of the trousers, as this permits greater ease in walking and is less liable to "give away" the method by causing the trouser-legs to vibrate during the dance. This manner of attaching the thread also makes it possible for the figure

Fig. 1.

to rise part way up and then fall back, as described above. This is done by unhooking one of the pins after the figure has been attached to the thread and manipulating it by hand while the performer bends forward to watch the sailor's movements, keeping the hand behind the calf of the leg to mask its movements.

The method of attaching the figure to the

thread, as given in *Modern Magic* and several other books, is to cut little slits in the cardboard at the sides of the head and bend them backward, thus forming little hooks which at the proper time engage the thread. I myself prefer to bend back the little ringlets at the sides of the head, which form equally effective hooks and make it possible to offer the figure for examination both before and after the performance.

THE SPIRIT COMMUNICATION

A QUESTION is written by one of the audience, placed in the smallest of a nest of four folded papers and given to the writer to hold. When the papers are unfolded, the slip bearing the question will have vanished, being replaced by a duplicate slip on which an answer is written.

For this, take two sheets of stiff paper of exactly the same size, say nine inches square, and fold them separately in three-inch folds each way, which will give you two packages three inches square and, if the folds have been carefully made, exactly alike. Then paste the backs of the middle portions of these together, making sure that the edges register exactly. Let them dry under a heavy weight, and you will then have a double package that looks like a single fold, either side of which can be opened. Inside *each* of these place a smaller fold and inside these still a smaller fold.

Enclose the whole in a ten-inch sheet folded in the same way.

On a sheet torn from a scratch pad write the following: "Looking at your question in one way the answer would unquestionably be 'Yes,' but from another point of view it is equally sure to be 'No.' This leaves your spirit control in a quandary, so she has taken your leaflet along to submit it to a higher authority, hoping to have the true answer at the next sitting." Fold this, place it in one of the smallest folds and make up the nest with the answer in the bottom part of the fake fold. You are now ready for the performance.

Begin by passing the scratch pad from which the answer has been torn to one of the company and ask that a question, the answer to which must be yes or no, be written upon it, the sheet torn off and so folded that it cannot be read.

Now open the nest on your table, leaving the sheets one on another in their proper order, and ask the writer to place the folded question in the smallest one. Then fold this as follows:

First the right hand side, then the left, then the fold nearest to you and, finally, the farthest. The next larger sheet is now folded in the same way, but the next is the fake and must be handled differently. In this case you fold the right, left, and nearest folds as before, but instead of finishing by folding the farthest *toward* you, you make the last fold *from* you, which turns the fake over and brings the answer uppermost.

The last sheet is folded fairly, like the unprepared ones, and the package passed to the writer to hold while the "spirit influence" is invoked. Finally, the package is placed on the table and all the folds are opened fairly and rapidly one upon the other. Then the answer, which will apply to any yes or no question, will be discovered.

THE KNIFE AND PAPER SLEIGHT

IF you cannot make a speech or sing a song and are not a success as a story-teller, you may still make an after-dinner hit if you know a few dinner-table tricks. The following is one of the best of this class.

Tear six pieces of paper about half an inch square, dampen them with water or wine, and stick them on the blade of a table knife, three on each side, about an inch and a half apart and as nearly opposite each other as possible.

Now remark that there is a great affinity between these bits of paper, so much so that when one is removed its partner vanishes also. To prove this take away the one nearest the handle, roll it into a pellet and throw it away. Show both sides of the knife: it will be seen that only two remain on each side. Remove another and show only one on each side. Finally, take away the last one and show both sides clean. Then say: "Hold on! I have just received a wireless message from the three partners, saying that they could not find their friends and are coming back. Oh, here they are!" Turn the knife over and reveal the three, showing both sides in succession several times, one having three papers and the other being clean. Stop with the papers uppermost and say: "Now I hear the others coming back." Show three on each side as at first. Show both sides several times and then stop suddenly and turn the ear to the knife, as if listening, and say: "Certainly, we'll excuse you." Then to the company: "The submerged partners say they have a date and must get away at once. Ah, there they go!" Turn the knife and show the under side clean. Pass it for examination with three on one side only.

The whole trick depends on a quick turn of the knife so that only one side is shown when the audience think they see both sides in succession. The twist can be learned in a few minutes and it cannot be detected if the instructions here given are followed.

After placing the six squares hold the knife with the blade near the surface of the table

and pointing away from your body. Grasp
the handle naturally with the lower part of
the end nearest the blade resting on the middle
joint of the forefinger, the thumb being on top.
To show the other side, bring the knife up
against your chest with the point of the blade
just below your chin. Repeat this three or
four times, then bring it down to the table and
take off the first square, after which you bring
the knife upward as before; but this time, during the upward movement, push your thumb
toward the point of the forefinger just far
enough to give the knife a half turn so that the
same side will be exposed, and when bringing
it downward reverse the twist. By this means
you can show either side at will and the effects
described above are easily obtained.

THE CHAMELEON CONFETTI

FIRST METHOD

FOR this an oblong box of thin wood or pasteboard is used, which is shown to be empty, also three bags of confetti, one red, one white and one blue. The confetti is poured into the box and thoroughly mixed, a handful being dropped on a plate to show that the mixture is complete. Another plate is now picked up and shown to be empty, and the audience is asked to name one of the colors. The performer immediately reaches into the box and brings out handful after handful of the chosen color and drops it on the plate, passing it for examination. The production of the other colors in the same way follows.

SECRET.—The box has two partitions hinged loosely at the bottom, so that they will either lie flat on the bottom or stand upright. (See Fig. 2.) When standing they are held in place by a weak spring. When the box is shown, the partitions lie on the bottom where, the inside of the box being dead black, they are invisible. Stand the box on the table and show the bags of confetti to be unmixed. Keeping the bags in sight, return to the table and again show the box empty, turning it over and rapping on the bottom with the wand to further

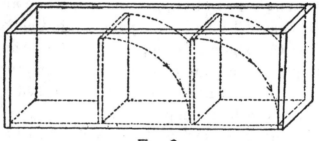

Fig. 2.

prove its emptiness. Of course when you turn it bottom up the partitions fall into an upright position, where they are held by the springs, and the box now has three compartments. The confetti is now poured into the box, one color into each compartment, and while you pretend to mix them, you retain a little of each color in the hand and drop it on the first plate. While walking toward the audience this is taken in the hand and dropped on the plate several times, seemingly to show it, and by this means it becomes thoroughly mixed.

Second Method

In this a glass box is used. The box stands on the table and is seen to be full of black con-

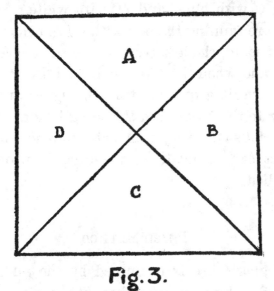

Fig.3.

fetti, a handful of which is taken openly from the box and thrown in the air to prove its color. The box is then fanned gently and the color changes to red, a handful being thrown out as before. Fanned again it is changed to blue, and finally to white, this being proved each time by a handful tossed in the air.

The secret of this is entirely in the glass box, which is divided as shown in Fig. 3. Division A is filled with black confetti; B with red; C with blue; and D, with white. While you are fanning the box with a fan held in the right hand, the left rests on the table near the box, and when the latter is hidden by the fan, you give it a quarter turn, bringing another color to the front, and the thing is done. This does not sound very wonderful to read, but the effect can be made very telling if properly handled.

Third Method

A glass vase is examined by the audience and filled by them with thoroughly mixed confetti: red, white, blue and black. The performer returns to his table and places the vase in plain sight of all, and on being asked for either color, takes up a handful, drops it on a plate and passes it for examination, when it is found to be of the chosen color. The other colors can be produced in any order called for.

For this effect the performer has concealed beneath his vest a package of confetti of each color, closely packed in a tissue paper cover of the same color. As he returns to the stage, he drops these into the vase, and it is then only necessary to pick up the color called for and squeeze it in the hand, thus breaking the covering, and let the contents fall on the plate.

An added effect is possible by having a duplicate package of one of the colors, red, for example, concealed behind some object on your table. Then, after the four colors have been produced, take the vase into the audience and show that the contents are still mixed as at first, return to the table, and set down the vase as if the trick were finished, at the same time picking up the extra package of confetti in the right hand and holding it concealed in the bend of the fingers. Then, say, as if by an afterthought, "Of course if somebody still wants red confetti, it is the easiest thing in the world to satisfy his desire." While speaking, pick up the plate with the left hand and reach into the vase with the right, producing the color as before.

PRODUCTION OF CONFETTI

THIS serves as a good introduction to the Water from Confetti effect.

The performer fills a tumbler with clear water and sets it on the table, after which he displays four pieces of different colored tissue paper and drops them into the water, stirring them about with the handle of a fan, and finally fishing them out with it. He takes them in the left hand, squeezes the water out and passes them to the right. Picking up the fan with the left hand, he fans the right, as if to complete the drying process, when a cloud of dry confetti is blown from the hand. Upon opening it, the wet sheets have vanished.

To produce this effect, make a small, closely packed bundle of confetti, confined in a tissue paper covering, and attach it to the back side of the fan at the top. Pick up the fan by this end and use the other to stir the paper sheets. After taking the paper in the left hand, lay down the fan, retaining the packet of confetti

49

in the right. Break the covering and fan out as above, rolling the wet sheets into as small a ball as possible and letting it drop to the floor. As the air is full of flying confetti the falling of the little ball will not be seen.

ANOTHER CONFETTI CHANGE

In this effect two ordinary glass tumblers are filled, one with red and the other with blue confetti, placed on a tray and passed for examination. Any person is at liberty to pour the confetti out upon the tray, one color at a time, of course, to prove that there is no preparation. The glasses are then wrapped in two pieces of newspaper, twisted at the top as in Fig. 4, and placed on separate tables. Show a little uncertainty and ask the audience which is which. This is sure to develop a difference in opinion, so, to make sure, tear a little hole in the side of each paper and reveal the color. Turn the glasses with these holes to the back after the audience is fully convinced of the location of each color.

Command the confetti to change places, remove the paper and show the changed position. Stand the tumblers on the tray as before and pass for examination.

51

EXPLANATION.—The pieces of newspaper
are about a foot square and are double, with
a small piece of clear celluloid between. On

Fig. 4.

one side of each piece of celluloid is pasted a
thin layer of confetti of the respective colors.
When wrapping the glasses, place the one con-

taining red confetti in the paper with the blue fake, and *vice versa,* being careful that the celluloid surface is toward the outside, and proceed as described above.

WATERED CONFETTI

In the well-known Indian Sand Trick the performer shows four or five saucers, each containing a handful of colored sand, pours the various colors into a bowl of water and, after they are thoroughly mixed, produces any color that the audience calls for, allowing it to flow from his hand in a perfectly dry state.

A variation of this effect in which confetti is used instead of sand is here explained for the first time in print.

A blown eggshell for each color is necessary, each of them being treated as follows: First stuff it full of confetti of a single color and seal the holes with waterproof cement. Then make a pellet of wet plaster of Paris a little larger than a pea, place it on a sheet of glass and press the side of the egg firmly into it. When this dries it will stick to the egg, but will come away from the glass, thus giving the egg a "foot" so that it will not roll about. Then dye the egg the same color as the confetti enclosed. Any of the analine dyes of commerce will serve for this. It should then be given a water resisting coating by being dipped quickly in and out of melted paraffin.

Place one of these eggs in the centre of each saucer, heap the confetti of the same color around it, and place the saucers in a semicircle around the front of the bowl. Show the bowl to be empty and unprepared, and fill it with clear water from a glass pitcher. Pour the confetti into the water, keeping the bottom of the saucers toward the audience, and note the position of each egg, so that it may be easily found. When all are in, mix the confetti and water thoroughly with your wand, being careful not to disturb the eggs, and while stirring the mixture with the right hand get hold of a handful of lycopodium with the left. As you finish stirring let this drop on the surface of the water, but do not try to stir it in. If you prefer you may do this openly, saying that it is a magic powder which causes the colors to separate. The lycopodium acts as a resistant to the water and the hand may now

be dipped into it and the chosen egg brought
out; the hand, the egg and the confetti being
alike bone dry.

Pick up one of the saucers with the other
hand and, holding it beneath, crush the shell
and allow the confetti to fall slowly into it.
When nearly all has fallen bring the hand
down and pick up half a handful and let it
drop on the saucer again, showing that it is
perfectly dry. In doing this drop the fragments of the shell behind the heaped confetti,
covering them with that which drops from the
hand.

Finish by producing the other colors in the
order called for. At the close a handful may
be taken in each hand and passed for examination, or it may be held on the open palm
and blown toward the audience.

THIS is an excellent little illusion and one that will prove the quality of the performer's showmanship. If given an artistic presentation it always makes a decided impression; if not so presented, it is flat and colorless.

First, pass for examination a solid ring of metal or wood, about twelve inches in diameter, and a Japanese paper napkin. Drop the ring over the head, letting it rest on the shoulder, return to your stage, crush up the napkin into a loose ball and lay it on the extended palm of the left hand. Make a few mesmeric passes over it with the right hand and after a moment it will slowly rise from the palm and float between the two hands.

Just here is the critical stage of the trick, for all depends on the graceful movements of the hands, which appear to influence the motions of the ball without contact, or with only an occasional contact of the tips of the fingers. Wave the hands above and below the ball to prove that it is not suspended by invisible wires, and take the ring from the neck and pass it backward and forward around it, thus seeming to prove that there is no connection anywhere. Drop the ring back over the head and after some further manipulation bring the ball back to the palm of the hand where it started, then, without making any suspicious movement with the hands, walk to the front and toss the ball into the audience.

The secret lies in the fact that the ball is made around a fine black thread, one end of which is fastened to a chair-back and the other terminates in a loop large enough to pass over the ear of the performer. This loop should be made by tying a *bow* slip-knot and leaving a hanging end two or three inches long with a pellet of magician's wax at the end. (See Fig. 5.)

This loop should lie on the table or in some easily accessible place, and, when the performer returns to the stage ofter the examination of the ring and napkin, he picks it up and slips it over his left ear, sticking the pellet of wax to the cheek just in front, and stands with his right side towards the audience. Standing away from the chair till the thread becomes taut, the slip knot is drawn down till the loop fits closely around the ear so that it cannot slip off.

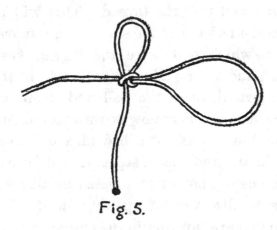

Fig. 5.

The napkin is now crushed into a ball *around the thread,* which has been allowed to slacken a little by the performer's moving nearer the chair, and placed on the palm. The movements of the ball are controlled by moving the head or bending the body nearer to, or further from, the chair. The sequence of moves I must leave to the ingenuity of the student.

At the finish, when making the passes with the right hand, which are supposed to cause the ball to settle on the left palm, bring the right hand up to the face, get hold of the pellet of wax and pull the thread. This will untie the bow-knot and at the same time remove the pellet, which will leave the thread free of knots; and as you advance to the front it will be drawn through the ball and drop to the floor. The ball may now be thrown out for examination. It is not a bad idea to leave the ring in the audience also, as it will be passed from one to another and tested in all sorts of ways to discover an opening in it. Later, when you are working in the audience on some other trick, it can be picked up.

THE JAPANESE BUTTERFLIES

It is a question whether this pretty effect should appear under the heading of Paper-tearing or under that of Paper tricks, as it shares a little the nature of both. In reality it is a feat of simple juggling, requiring but little skill after the "knack" has been acquired. The apparatus is inexpensive, consisting of a little silk paper and a couple of blonde hairs.

It is purely a Japanese production and very few European performers have made use of it, but if properly presented it can be made highly entertaining. Anderson, the Wizard of the North, is credited with its introduction into America.

Some performers open the act with the butterflies already made, but to my mind it is much more effective to first show two pieces of paper and begin by tearing and folding them into the proper shape.

By using the fan with the right hand, the

butterflies can be made to rise from the palm of the left, hover about the performer in the most natural manner, follow him wherever he goes, and light on the edge of a fan, or upon a bouquet of flowers taken from the table. In fact, the ingenuity of the performer will suggest many natural movements for the little moths.

PREPARATION FOR THE EFFECT.—When the butterflies are to be torn on the stage, take two oblong pieces of silk paper, a little larger than a cigarette paper, and attach one end of an eighteen-inch blonde hair to the centre of one of the long sides of each. To the centre of this hair tie another, 25 or 30 inches long, as shown at *A* in Fig. 6, and at the other end, *B,* attach a pellet of magician's wax. When you are ready to go on the stage, attach the pellet to one side of the forehead at the edge of the hair where it will not be seen. (See Fig. 7.) Then take the two pieces of paper in the right hand, being careful not to snarl the hairs, and with the fan under the arm, walk down to the front and show the squares of paper, which will seem to be unprepared, as the hair is quite invisible even at close range.

Now, fold the paper together as shown in Fig. 8, the hair being fastened at the point marked x, tear out the butterfly as shown, and proceed as above.

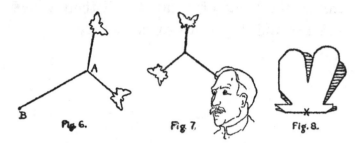

Fig. 6.   Fig 7.   Fig. 8.

Do not be discouraged if the butterflies seem to have wills of their own at first and go anywhere but to the places you desire, for there is certainly a knack in handling the fan which cannot be explained and can be acquired only by experiment; but once you have mastered this, the movement of the butterflies can be controlled to a nicety that will surprise even yourself.

Many years ago, at an entertainment in New York, I saw an old-timer who was quite successful with this effect for which he used a slightly different method. He attached a small bead to the end of the hair and held this in his mouth, but it can be transferred to the hand or to a pocket if desired at any time. He finished by making the butterflies hover around the flame of a candle till their wings took fire and they were consumed.

THE SHAVING STICK

Somebody gave me this combination so long ago that I have forgotten who it was, but I have never seen it performed, and I suggest working it about as follows. In this form it should fit nicely into a parlor program.

Pick up a shaving stick box like *B* in Fig. 9 and, while unscrewing the cover, say, "I have here a number of coins . . . " Tip the box over the left hand; instead of coins a shaving stick drops out. Lay the stick on the table and step forward with the box, saying, "This is rather embarrassing! The fact is I have one of these boxes in which I keep a set of coins; as you see, it is just the size for a half-dollar." Let the audience take the box and the coin, ostensibly to show the fit of the coin; they will take occasion to examine the box and cover at the same time. Note that they are not asked to examine it; if they were, they might notice that they have had no opportunity to examine the stick.

Continue, "In my hurry I picked up the wrong box, so my coins are at home. However, I have the box, so I must do some kind of a trick with it." After a moment of thought, take a box of mixed confetti that has been used in another trick, fill the box, blow off the surplus confetti from the top, screw on the cover and set it down near someone in the audience, asking that it be watched so that the confetti cannot escape. Return to your table and pick up the stick with the right hand and a fan with the left. Fan the right hand and a great cloud of confetti will be blown from it. When it is opened the stick will have vanished.

The person who was asked to watch the box is now requested to unscrew the cover. On doing so he finds that the confetti has disappeared. In its place is the shaving stick, which completely fills the box.

EXPLANATION.—Take the cover of a shaving-stick box in which the lettering is stamped in the metal, as shown in *A,* Fig. 9, and cut away the sides, leaving a disk just large enough to fit tightly inside another cover of the same kind.

(See *B.*) Glue to the top surface of this disk a thin layer of confetti. Then make an imitation shaving stick out of whitish-brown paper of the color of the soap, covering the lower part with tin-foil like the ordinary stick, fill this with closely packed confetti and load it into an unprepared shaving-stock box.

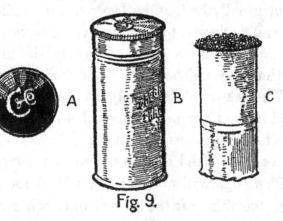

Fig. 9.

Wet the top of a new shaving stick and press the confetti-covered disk on it with the confetti side up, as in *C,* till the wet soap sets, when it will hold almost as firmly as if glued. Conceal this in the box of mixed confetti and you are ready for the performance.

Fill the box once or twice, letting the confetti flow back into the larger box, and finally load in the stick, the disk giving it the appearance of a full box. When the cover is screwed on it twists the disk off the top of the stick and wedges it tightly into the top of the cover, so that when the custodian of the box unscrews the top the inside has exactly the appearance it originally had, and all seems fair to him. It is well, however, to get the cover into your own hands as soon as possible, so that the investigation may not be carried too far.

The fake stick is simply crushed in the hand and broken open, the pieces being dropped to the floor with the confetti.

A needle-sized hole in the cover through the milled edge will not be seen, and by means of this the fake can be forced out; otherwise it will be difficult to remove it.

THIS very pretty production trick was in
De Kolta's program during his first engage-
ment at the Eden Musée. This was, I think,
its first showing in America.

De Kolta first displayed a number of pieces
of different colored tissue paper about six
inches square. These he rolled into a small
ball and suddenly in place of them his hands
were filled with little paper flags, each on a
staff. As he walked through the audience the
flags multiplied marvellously and he scattered
them in all directions, the supply seeming to
be inexhaustible.

The flags used by De Kolta were of tissue
paper, about an inch and a half by two inches
in size, and the staffs were of broom straw.
They were made up in packets of a hundred
or more and for compactness half were laid
in one direction and half in the other. The
packets were wrapped in black tissue paper
with the ends open, and disposed in different

pockets. The first in a little pocket just inside the opening of the coat on the right side. To this a black thread was attached and the other end fastened to the lapel of the vest. In showing the paper squares the left thumb was hooked over the thread, the packet brought behind the squares, the black paper broken and the flags produced.

While walking through the audience and bending over to throw flags to distant seats, other packets were taken from under the lapel of the coat, from beneath the vest and other handy hiding places.

Later performers used much larger flags on wooden staffs, with their professional cards printed on them.

THE PIG AND THE RING

READERS of Professor Hoffmann's *Later Magic* may recall a trick in which a handkerchief is changed to paper shavings. The invention is there credited to Herr Camill Bihler, a German conjuror. Many different combinations have been founded on this little trick, and the following, which I modestly claim as my own, is one that can be worked anywhere and has an excellent "punch" at the finish.

The effect is as follows: Standing on your table is a pasteboard box, say, twelve inches long, eight inches wide and six deep, two-thirds full of paper clippings of mixed colors; also an empty glass tumbler, a colored handkerchief, a small piece of flash paper and a paper cylinder about six inches in height, open at both ends and of sufficient size to be slipped loosely over the tumbler.

First show the cylinder, holding it in an

upright position, and say, "I have here a paper bag without top or bottom and quite empty, as you see." To "prove" this statement, pass your wand down through the cylinder very carefully, as if avoiding something hidden therein. This will have the effect of convincing many of the company that it is far from empty, and, pretending to hear a protest, you bring the wand up to the horizontal with the cylinder hanging on it, so that all can see completely through it. Whirling the cylinder on the wand a few times, you remark, "I think you folks are over-particular. If you insist upon seeing through everything, how can I hope to surprise you?"

Go back to your table and bring forward the box, leaving the cylinder standing on the table. Tip the box forward so that they can see the clippings, take out a handful, toss them in the air and then place the box on a side table.

Pick up the handkerchief and throw it across the left arm and then take the tumbler, saying, "Here's something else that you can see through. As you see, empty on the inside and empty on the outside, except for an invisible combination of oxygen and other gases without which it would be impossible for me to continue the experiment." Fill the tumbler with clippings and pour back into the box two or three times to show that all is perfectly fair, and the last time blow away the heaped clippings from the top, cover it with the handkerchief, step forward and say, "I will now pass the tumbler and its contents into the paper bag there on the table. Shall I do it visibly or invisibly?" Whatever the answer, shake out the handkerchief from which both glass and clippings have vanished. Cross to the table and lift the cylinder, showing the glass full of clippings, which you pour into the box. Set the empty tumbler beside it.

Continue your patter by saying, "You may think that these things travel in this remarkable manner because they belong to me. To disprove this I should like to use something of your own. Will some kind lady loan me a wedding ring? Don't be afraid to trust me with it, for I almost always return the articles

which I borrow." Have the lender slip the
ring on the point of your wand, return to your
table and lay down the wand with the ring still
on it. Now fill the tumbler with clippings
again, place it on the table and cover with the
cylinder. Wrap the ring in the flash paper
and toss it in the air, where it vanishes in a
burst of flame. Immediately lift the cylinder
and it will be seen that the clippings have vanished and in their place is a guinea-pig. Bring
the glass and the cylinder forward without
touching the pig and the owner of the ring will
find her property tied by a ribbon around the
neck of the pig.

A description of the properties and their
uses will give a pretty clear idea of the working of the trick. They are as follows: First,
three clear glass tumblers, all alike, with
nearly straight sides. Second, a box of paper
clippings, as described above. Third, a cardboard shell shaped to fit inside one of the
tumblers, filling it completely. The bottom of
the shell is open and an opening half an inch
wide extends up one side to within half an inch

of the top. The top is closed by a disk of cardboard which projects about an eighth of an inch all around, so that it can be gripped and carried away with the cylinder. Paper clippings are glued all over the outside of the shell, so that when it is in the tumbler the latter appears to be full of clippings. Inside this shell a guinea-pig is loaded. Around his neck is a ribbon tied in a bow-knot, the bows of which are four inches long and are allowed to protrude through the opening in the side of the shell. This is now loaded into one of the tumblers with the ribbon bows hanging outside, and thus loaded the tumbler is concealed under the clippings in the box. Fourth, a paper cylinder, as described. Fifth, a double handkerchief inside which a ring of the size of the top of the tumbler is so arranged that it will drop into one of the corners or into the centre, as desired. A good description of this handkerchief will be found in Hoffmann's *Modern Magic,* page 370. Sixth, a piece of flash paper, which may be procured from any dealer in magical apparatus. Fold a hem about a quarter of an inch wide along one edge of the paper and glue it down, thus making a little tube along one side. Close one end of this tube with glue and drop into it a little flash powder, which is made by mixing equal parts of chlorate of potash and sugar of milk, and slip in an acid tube and seal up the other end. The acid tubes are needle-sized glass tubes filled with sulphuric acid, and can be found at any magic store.

At the beginning, the third tumbler, filled with paper clippings, stands behind the box on the table. After the cylinder has been shown empty, drop it over the glass of clippings while picking up the box. This will not be noticed, as the two moves are made simultaneously and the cylinder is left on the table in full sight.

When the first glass is filled from the box, it is held in the left hand just above the box and covered with the handkerchief. The right hand then seizes the ring, which appears to be the top of the tumbler, and the left hand lowers the tumbler and leaves it in the box, and that part of the trick is finished as described above.

The borrowed ring is on the point of the wand as described in the Ring and Program, on page 10. After getting possession of the borrowed ring you fill the tumbler with clippings two or three times as before, and while doing this, slip the ring over one of the bows of ribbon hanging from the loaded glass, passing the end of the bow over the ring; the latter will then be tied fast to the bow. When filling the tumbler for the last time, leave it in the box and bring up the loaded glass instead, being careful that the opening and the hanging ring are on the side away from the audience.

Now, cover the loaded tumbler with the cylinder, pick up the wand, slide the dummy ring off and wrap it in the flash paper. As you toss it in the air, break the tube with the fingers and the flash follows.

When you lift the cylinder from the tumbler all eyes will be on the guinea-pig, thus giving you an opportunity to let the shell drop from the cylinder into the box. You can then carry the empty cylinder with you when you take the tumbler to the owner of the ring.

COFFEE, MILK AND SUGAR

THIS belongs to that class of tricks which, while old in years of service, is, if artistically presented, ever new to an audience. It was one of the favorites of our dean, Harry Kellar,* and in a different form figured in the programs of those never-to-be-forgotten artists, Imro Fox and Chung Ling Soo.

In the Kellar version a light wooden box half full of white paper clippings was shown, a handful of which he tossed in the air with that well-remembered expression, "Papier blanco"; then a like box of blue clippings, introduced as "Papier bleu"; finally, a box of bran. A nickeled cocktail shaker was then produced, shown to be quite empty, and filled with the white clippings. This was placed on a side table and covered with a little square of

---

* Regret to say that since writing this book, Dean Kellar passed away, in Los Angeles, March 10, 1922. In the near future I hope to be able to publish his biography, on which I have been working for several years. Dean Kellar was an ornament to the world of magic.—H. H.

black velvet. Another like vessel was filled with the blue clippings, placed on another table and covered in the same way; and finally, a glass jar was filled with bran and covered with a paper cylinder.

After a few mesmeric passes the velvet cover was removed from the first shaker and it was found to be full of steaming hot coffee; the second was full of milk, and when the cylinder was lifted from the glass jar it was full of cut loaf sugar.

EXPLANATION.—In the boxes of white and blue clippings were concealed duplicate shakers, one filled with coffee and the other with milk. These were furnished with metal covers upon which paper clippings of the respective colors were pasted, and while pretending to fill the others the performer exchanged them for these, which appeared to be full of clippings. At one side of each of these covers a little ear of the metal projected and in the act of covering with the velvet squares the cover was lifted by this ear, carried back and dropped on the servante.

For the bran a shell of metal of the shape and size to fit loosely in the glass jar, with the top closed by a disk having a projecting flange and the bottom open was used. This shell was covered with a coating of bran so that when in the jar it had the appearance of being full of bran. The shell, filled with sugar, stood bottom up in one corner of the box of bran and was loaded into the jar when the performer was pretending to fill it. When the cylinder was lifted from this the flange was pinched through the paper and the shell carried away with it and dropped into the box of bran.

A good finish for this trick when it is performed in a parlor is to have a tray with a sufficient number of after-dinner coffee cups to supply the whole company, and serve them all with hot coffee. If the company is too large for the supply of coffee, a little warm water should be previously placed in each cup.

In the form of this trick used by Fox, Soo and others, the velvet squares were dispensed with. They passed for examination the two cocktail shakers and two shallow metal lids for the same. The duplicate shakers were covered with loosely fitting covers with a coating of clippings, and as the lids fitted closely over these, they were carried away also when the latter were removed. Full sets of this apparatus will be found at any magical emporium.

Fox used to finish by pouring out a cup of coffee and, when about to drink it, pretending to change his mind and throwing the contents out into the audience; instead of a shower of hot coffee it proved to be a cupful of blue and white clippings. This was accomplished by means of a cup with a false bottom, all the coffee passing into the hollow saucer.

THE BALLOT OR PELLET TEST

OF all the tricks ever conceived wherein paper serves as a vehicle, the greatest from every standpoint is the Pellet, or, as it is sometimes called, the Ballot, Test, its names being taken from the terminology of the spirit mediums, who for many years have found it to be a positive gold mine. Fortunes have been built and are still being amassed on this trick alone.

In my travels over the face of the earth I have met hundreds of both professional and amateur workers of this marvellous delusion, and I am free to say that no trick that I have ever seen gives such an impression of openness and simplicity in execution and at the same time such startling results.

The best amateur performance of the test I ever witnessed was given by John Ringling, of circus fame, and by far the best professional demonstration was by Dr. Reiss.

The usual method of presentation is to distribute a number of slips of paper about the

size of cigarette papers and ask the company
to write any question they please and then fold
the papers into small squares. Sometimes
these are collected in a hat and sometimes they
are thrown openly on the table; then, without
any apparent opportunity of seeing what is
written, the medium either repeats or gives
some sort of answer to the questions.

The side of the trick which the audience sees
differs widely in the work of different exponents, but the fundamental principle is the
same in all cases. The one great necessity is to
get possession of, and read, the first pellet.
After that the game is easy.

In the earlier form of the trick the medium
collected all the pellets in a hat, and while
walking to his table stole one of them, got it
open and dropped it in the hat face upward.
He then placed the hat on the table, and showing his hand to be quite empty, reached in and
took one of the pellets and held it against his
forehead. While doing this he read the exposed pellet. Then he closed his eyes and
slowly repeated the question that he had just

seen. When someone acknowledged the question he opened the pellet, apparently to see if he had repeated it correctly, but really to read the question on that one, tossed it on the table and took another from the hat, and so on till all were read. While taking the others from the hat he had ample opportunity to re-fold the first one, this being taken last. Of course, all the pellets being vouched for, the mystery was very deep.

Another much less artistic method is to have one of the questions written by a confederate. In this case some method of identification is necessary, so that the planted question can be spotted and left till the last. At the close all the pellets are left unfolded on the table so that anyone may inspect them, but of course it is impossible to discover which was the first selected.

The best form of the test, however, and one calling for expertness of the highest order, is the individual sitting. Here only the medium and the sitter are present, and there are men who work these sittings so cleverly that even when the victim knows the game in a general way, it is impossible for him to follow the manipulations.

The visitor is asked to sit at a square-cornered table which stands in the centre of the room, and to write five or six questions on separate slips of paper, fold them four times and leave them on the table. The medium usually picks up a sheet of paper and tears it into ballots about the size of cigarette papers, sees that the sitter has a pen or pencil and then either leaves the room or goes to some point where it is impossible for him to see what is written, asking that he be called when the ballots are written and folded. He generally folds one to show how the four folds should be made.

When recalled, the medium seats himself at the opposite side of the table, picks up a pellet at random, places it against the forehead of the sitter, who is asked to hold it there with his left hand and to place his right on the medium's head, while the latter places his own left hand on the head of the sitter, a position which is supposed to establish the necessary magnetic connection. The medium then "concentrates," massaging his brow with his free right hand, rolling his eyes, or indulging in any other hocus-pocus that he thinks will impress his sitter. After a time he decides that the connection is not perfect, and asks the sitter to hold the pellet against his, the medium's, forehead. There is still something wrong and he concludes that the personal contact will not succeed in this case, so he asks the sitter to hold the pellet in his own left hand or to put it in his pocket. After another period of "concentration," he repeats and answers the question.

In this case the reading is obtained by a sleight-of-hand switch of the pellets. When the medium seats himself at the table he holds concealed between the points of the first and second fingers of the left hand a blank ballot. This is folded as nearly as possible like those on the table, one of which he picks up with the same hand. Just as he is about to place it against the sitter's forehead, and while the fingers are out of his range of vision, the blank is pushed forward and the written pellet drawn back into its place, so that the sitter holds the blank. The hand is then rested on the sitter's head and the magnetic connection completed as above. The medium now opens the pellet with the left hand, reads the question, refolds and conceals it as before. He can take his time about this, as it is supposed that several minutes of concentration are necessary. There is no possible way for the sitter to detect this move, as the *back* of the hand rests on his head and the medium has taken the precaution to provide soft paper that will not "talk" while being unfolded. The blank pellet is now transferred to the medium's forehead and, when that position proves to be a failure, he reaches up and takes the pellet with the fingers of the right hand, which allows the sitter to see that this hand is quite empty, and passes it to the fingers of the left, where the written pellet is concealed, holding it in such a way that fully two-thirds of it is in sight. He then looks up suddenly and says, for instance, "You are not getting tired, are you?"

The sitter involuntarily raises his eyes; in a fraction of a second the switch is made and the written pellet is passed to him to hold in his left hand or to place in his pocket.

Many other methods of reading the pellet are in use. It can be opened with the left hand and palmed while the sitter is being instructed how to hold the duplicate against his forehead, read and refolded to be switched later, or dropped in the lap and read at leisure. In fact, since the sitter thinks he is holding the pellet himself, this part of the test is by no means difficult. The switch is the big idea and it must be practised until the execution is perfect, otherwise the trick will fail.

A very clever dodge, by means of which the question is read although the medium's eyes are seen to be closed throughout the period of concentration, was explained to me some time ago by an old-time medium. He got the pellet open and held it in his hand near his thigh, concealed from the sitter by the table; then with his eyes tightly closed he rolled his head from side to side and when his profile was presented to the visitor he opened his "off eye" and read the question.

Another method and one that I found very useful when I gave the test was to take a pellet haphazard from those on the table and, after holding it against my forehead for a little time, pretend to read a very silly question, a question that anyone might hesitate to answer in public. After waiting for an answer and receiving none, I would open the pellet and, glancing at it, say: "Yes, that's right," and repeat the question. Still getting no answer, I would say: "If you do not acknowledge your questions it is useless for me to proceed. I will read two more questions and if the writers do not claim them I shall go no farther." As I now had the first question memorized, the remainder of the test was eminently successful. I did not use a hat, but had the pellets thrown openly on the table.

For one entire season, 1918, I made a 10,000-pound elephant—Jenny, daughter of Jumbo—vanish twice daily at the New York Hippodrome. If that can be done without detection, it should be easy to get away with a half-inch pellet.

Confederates are also used and very wonderful tests result, as the coadjutor will say "Yes" to anything.

It is important to note all the following carefully, as this is the greatest method of all.*

Some of the modern exponents first get the contents of all the pellets and memorize them. They then have the sitter place one in each vest pocket and the others in different spots about the room, the medium keeping track of them all. He then asks which shall be read and answered, and, after a proper amount of hesitation, he succeeds in reading and answering the one selected. The latter test has fooled some of the greatest minds in the world. A well-known performer who used this test suc-

---

* This is one of the methods used by Dr. Reiss, who is, in my estimation, the greatest pellet reader that ever lived. I had a seance with Dr. Reiss, and if it had not been for my many years experience as an expert, I might have been mystified by his adroit manipulations and uncanny deductions. It is subtle misdirection, maneuvering, and bold presentation, and from my personal contact with him I haven't the slightest hesitancy in saying there is nothing abnormal or telepathic in his method.

cessfully for years told me that he kept track of the different memorized pellets by means of a system of markings made with his thumb nail while refolding them.

In the above description I have by no means exhausted the possibilities of this wonderful confidence game, but have given the main features only, knowing that any reader who is clever enough to succeed with it will also be clever enough to invent a series of moves fitted to his own capabilities.

PAPER CLIPPINGS AND WATER

A NEW way to use an old piece of apparatus is always desirable. The following trick, which has never appeared in print before, should therefore be a welcome newcomer.

In performing this, first show a cardboard cylinder about five inches high and two in diameter, also a ring of the same material about three-fourths of an inch wide and large enough to slip easily over the cylinder. After these have been examined, place a piece of tissue paper over one end of the cylinder and slip the ring over it, thus giving it a sort of drum-head, and tear off the superfluous paper below the ring. While returning to your table keep the cylinder in sight of the audience, so that they may see that it is not loaded in any way.

Fill the cylinder with colored paper clippings from a box on the table and pour back into the box to show that the tube is really filled with the clippings and nothing else. Fill it again and stand it on the bottom of an inverted glass tumbler. Now tear a piece about six or seven inches square from a newspaper, place the centre of it on the top of the cylinder and press it down around the sides, thus forming a sort of tent-shaped cover. Lift this cover up and show the cylinder still full of clippings, drawing attention to the fact that the tumbler is never covered and only the upper part of the cylinder is hidden by the paper.

Announce that you will now cause the clippings to pass back into the box invisibly. Then go to the box and take out a handful, saying, "You see there is no deception, for those who were particular to notice the clippings which were in the cylinder may easily recognize these as the identical fragments." Remove the paper and show that the clippings have vanished. Then twist the paper up to show that there is nothing in it and toss it into the audience.

Going back to the cylinder, glance into it and say, "I can see that there are still a few bits of paper here and I will now show you what a wonderful effect a little water will have on them." From a small glass pitcher pour about a wineglassful of water into the cylinder and wait a moment for the promised effect. As nothing happens, you say, "Something seems to be wrong. I'll pour the water out and try again." Invert the cylinder over the pitcher, but as no water appears you say, "Hello, what has become of the water?" Look the tube over carefully and then say, "I wonder if it could get out of the bottom. Tear the tissue paper away, saying, "Still no water, but I can see that it has been used up in joining the clippings into one long ribbon." Draw out paper ribbon and reel it up on the hand, the colors being the same as those of the clippings.

When the ribbon is exhausted you can show the cylinder quite empty and it may be examined if desired.

EXPLANATION.—For this effect a tin tube, constructed as shown in Fig. 10, is used. The inside of the top is funnel-shaped, as shown by the dotted lines, with a hole in the centre, so that water may be poured into it, but cannot be poured out. The bottom is open, but there

is a bottom for the inner part a little over
half an inch above, as shown by dotted lines,
and in the centre of this is an opening which
is plugged by a cork as shown. This is for
the purpose of letting the water out when it is

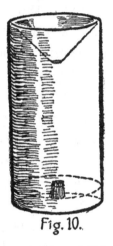

Fig. 10.

not in use. The outside of this tube is covered
with strips of paper ribbon pasted haphazard
over its surface, and in the space at the bottom
is a roll of paper ribbon of the same colors as
the clippings. This must fit tightly, so that it
will not drop out, and the end of the inner coil
drawn out a little, so as to be easily get-at-able.

The cylinder is of light cardboard, about an

inch taller than the tube and just large enough to slip easily over it. A cover for this is made from a disk of tin about a sixteenth of an inch larger than the diameter of the cylinder, with a lip on the under side to keep it from slipping out of place. On the top side a thin layer of clippings is pasted, so that when it is placed on the top the cylinder appears to be full of clippings. Both the tube and the cover are concealed in the box of clippings.

After filling the cylinder two or three times, as described above, slip the tube into the cylinder, place the cover on top, lift out the apparently full cylinder, place it on the tumbler and cover with the square of paper, as described. While putting on the paper the second time with the right hand, palm off the cover with the left. This is very easy, as the cover is about the size of a silver dollar and the paper masks the move. The cover can be dropped into the box.

Now follow the original description, which needs no further explanation till you come to the point where the ribbon is exhausted. As is usual in paper ribbon productions, the hand should make wide sweeps, first one way and then the other, coiling and mixing the paper in a very effective manner, the tube being held inside the cylinder by pinching it; but just as the end of the ribbon is reached and while the sweep of the hand brings the coils below the cylinder, remove the pressure and allow the tube to fall into the coils where its colors mix with the others and it cannot be seen. Drop the coiled ribbon on the box of clippings; show the empty cylinder and—take your applause.

WERNER'S BILL TEARING TRICK

EVERYBODY familiar with magic and magicians in New York City has seen Francis J. Werner's Bill Tearing Trick. In his competent hands this effect is little short of a masterpiece of magic, and notwithstanding the tendency of the times toward stealing the other fellow's best tricks, a general policy of "hands-off" seems to have been adopted in this case, and he has had a practical monopoly of this effect for years.

Mr. Werner has given me permission to include his own version of the trick in the present volume, so I will pass it along to you with such of his patter as is necessary to make it plain.

The effect consists in tearing a bank-note into small bits and restoring it to its original form. For good measure the tearing and restoration is repeated and at the end the bill is found to be none the worse for its double destruction.

A duplicate bill is necessary and this should be crumpled into a loose ball and concealed in the bend of the left elbow, or under the edge of the vest at the right side. This bill is palmed in the right hand while returning to the stage after borrowing the marked bill from the audience. Werner sometimes varies this by taking a roll of bills from his own pocket and remarking that he has money of his own, but prefers to borrow rather than to risk it. In replacing the roll in his pocket he palms off one bill, crumples it up and holds it in his right hand.

Several bills are usually proffered and it is best to accept one on your right if possible. The reason for this will appear as the trick develops. Pass a pencil to the lender and ask him to mark the bill for identification. When he returns it, say: "The pencil first, please, as I do not wish to have anything in my hands but your bill." The pencil is replaced in the pocket before the bill is accepted.

Francis J. Werner

IN WHOSE HANDS THE BILL-TEARING TRICK IS A CLASSIC

Then turn to someone on the left and ask him to take the number of the bill, writing it on a card or the edge of his program, and say to him: "This is in justice to me and to prevent substitution." After retiring to the stage lay the bill on the palm of the open right hand, which will conceal the duplicate palmed there, and carelessly show the left hand to be empty. Continue the patter by saying: "Some people flash their money like drunken sailors, in which case they are often approached for a loan, and if the request comes from a friend there is no excuse for refusing him, even if this one bill is all you have, so you offer him half, like this." Bring the two hands together and seize the top of the bill in the middle with the thumbs and fingers of both hands and turn the top slightly towards the body, so that it may not be torn during the next move, also to prevent cutting the right forefinger on the edge if the bill happens to be stiff. Now make a downward movement with the right hand, as if tearing the bill through the centre, but really allowing the fingers to slip over it, which

will make a sound identical with that of tearing, and at the same time bend the right-hand
end toward the left and seize it with the last
three fingers of that hand, crumpling it up
into a ball—the bill will curl over the index
finger of the left hand, which will make this
move easy—then bring both hands rapidly up
before the chest and show the crumpled pieces
(?) in each hand.

A laugh may be raised here by saying:
"This is the reason that I never use my own
money. Should your friend desire less than
half, again tear the bill making quarters, or
eighths, or sixteenths, and so on." Each time
you rub the two balls together as if tearing,
and finally leave the duplicate safely palmed
in the left hand. Now remark that you allow
your thumb-nails to grow long in order to
make this final tear, and make this tear appear rather difficult.

You now have the borrowed bill in a small
ball at the tips of the fingers of the left hand
and the duplicate palmed in the same. You

should now go to the person who took the number of the bill and ask him to examine the pieces and see if they are sufficiently small.

Great care should be exercised in executing the next move, as the eyes of all will be upon you. As you pass the borrowed bill—the supposed pieces—with your left hand, palm downward, instantly advance your right hand underneath the one in which he receives the bill and quickly bring your left hand under the right, thus covering the palmed duplicate, at the same time saying: "Be careful not to drop any of the pieces." While the crumpled bill is being opened and all are watching it, slowly withdraw your hands and get rid of the duplicate by slipping it into a pocket at the first opportunity, so that both hands shall be empty when you take back the bill, with the remark: "You find the pieces all intact, or in other words, the bill fully restored."

After having the bill identified by the owner, say: "I will now show you how it is done, but don't tell any member of the Society of

American Magicians, as their laws forbid the exposure of any magical effects, and it might cost me my membership.''

No duplicate is used in the second part of the trick. Return to the stage and hold the bill in the left hand, palm toward the body, and the bill hanging downward parallel to the body, the right hand being shown empty without comment.

Then say: ''In performing this feat do not make any rapid movements or you will be suspected of hiding something.'' Then slowly show the right hand, back and front, and, taking the bill from the left, show that hand in the same way. Now let your right hand rest against the bottom of your vest as if you were taking something therefrom. Such an open movement would be unpardonable in a magician and your audience will be sure to suspect it, but proceed as if you were unconscious of the suspicion, explaining that the skeptic sometimes wants to see both sides of the bill at once. Make the following moves as if concealing something behind the bill.

"I satisfy the skeptic by showing both sides thus." Turn one of the lower corners of the bill over against the front, showing a part of the back, and let it fall back into place. "This should satisfy him." Now pass the bill from the left to the right hand and back several times, showing the respective hands empty each time, but making the change as if holding something behind the borrowed bill, and a little good acting here will convince your audience that such is the case. Someone is quite likely to ask to see both hands; if not, you can assume that you are suspected and say: "Some of you appear to think that I have another bill concealed here, but you should know that I would not do anything like that."

Here you extend your left hand palm downward, place the bill on the back of that hand and slowly open the right, showing it to be quite empty.

Now proceed with the tearing movement as before, except that it is done much more rapidly, and no duplicate being used, the insides of the hands are not shown. Continue to tear into quarters, eighths and so on as before, the rapid movement making it impossible to detect that there is nothing in the right hand. Finally, take the crumpled bill in the right hand and, showing the left empty, extend that hand and place the crumpled bill on the palm. Explain that this—moving the open right hand three times over the fragments—means everything. You now smooth out the bill and show it fully restored. Return it to the owner who will identify it as the one he marked; take your applause and bow as if you knew that you had earned it.

Above all be cheerful when presenting this mystification. The charm of Werner's presentation lies in the sardonically gleeful way in which he apparently tears the bill in pieces.

The patter used here is original with Werner, but the student should use language suited to his own personality and the general trend of his program.

The magical fraternity owe the singing magician a "thank you" for having given

them .a method which is the result of years
of observation and study. The reason Werner
is called the singing magician is that he pos-
sesses a robust barytone voice.

AN EFFECTIVE FINISH

IT is always desirable to secure a telling effect to close an act. For this purpose, in the case of a paper act, I suggest the following as a sure-fire applause producer.

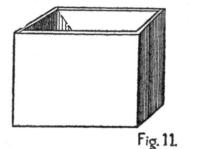

Fig. 11.

The performer introduces a pasteboard box about twelve inches square and eight deep, half full of mixed red, white and blue confetti, also a pasteboard cylinder about two and a half inches in diameter and five inches long, with a slip cover which fits tightly over one end. (See Fig. 11.)

After having these examined, he holds the cylinder over the box and pours a few handfuls of confetti through it. Then, putting the cover on one end, he proceeds to fill the tube with confetti. Leveling off the heaped confetti with the top of the tube, he steps forward and draws up from the open end a silk flag attached to a pole three or four feet high, having spiral red, white and blue stripes, like a barber-pole. After waiting a moment for applause, he contiuues to extend the pole upwards till it reaches a height of thirty or forty feet. (See Fig. 12.)

EXPLANATION. — Two tubes and covers are used, one being unprepared and the other arranged as follows: Procure a *double roll* of wallpaper which has a pure white back, and cut it into four pieces. This will give you four small rolls four and a half inches long, each roll containing fifty-four feet. You will need only one and the others may be put aside for future use. Paint a red stripe along one edge

Fig. 12

of the white side about an inch and a quarter wide, leave the same width white and paint the balance blue. With a flat brush and red and blue inks of strong color, the painting is easy. When it is thoroughly dry roll the strip up on a five-eighth inch dowel as tightly as possible. After the roll is made it should be laid on the table, rolled over and over, and pressed rather heavily with the hands, by which means the roll can be made very tight indeed. The tube should be of such diameter as to allow this roll to fit closely inside, where it should be fastened with glue, the top being about one-quarter of an inch below the top of the cylinder. Now push out the dowel, leaving an opening in which to pack the flag. The top of the flag should be fastened to the inside fillet of the roll and the bottom to a rather heavy ring. Push the flag into the roll, leaving the ring on top so that when the pole is pulled up the point will pass through it and it will drop down and hold the bottom corner of the flag in place.

The prepared tube should be in the bottom

of the box, covered with the confetti, so as not to be seen when the box is shown. When filling the other tube it is easy to make the exchange and bring up the loaded one with a handful of confetti heaped on the top, which, when leveled off, leaves just enough to cover the end of the roll, so that all looks fair and square.

Now you have only to pull up the inside fillet of the roll *through the ring* and the flag will follow and settle into place. Then develop the remainder of the pole as described above.

PART TWO
PAPER FOLDING

THE JAPANESE BIRD

In the days before the cabaret New York boasted a considerable number of popular dining clubs which brought together a host of people who could "do entertaining things." At one of these dinners I observed an Americanized Japanese folding a leaf of the menu card in a peculiar manner. Gradually all those within "seeing distance" became interested, and before he finished he was quite surrounded by spectators who applauded him roundly when, from that scrap of pasteboard, he at last produced a little paper bird that flapped its wings quite naturally.

Since then the clever Jap has taught me how to make the bird. Here is the trick: Take a square piece of letter paper six inches or more in size and fold from corner to corner in each direction and then across the centre both ways, making all the folds sharp in order that they may serve as guides in the further folding. The sheet will then appear as in Fig.

13. Now fold the side *a, h, g,* over to the line
a, e, as in Fig. 14, and sharpen the fold from

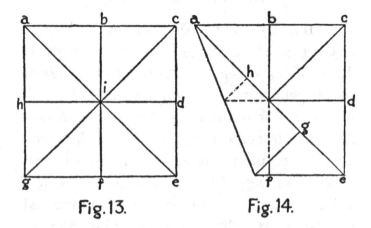

Fig. 13.   Fig. 14.

a to *h only,* merely bending the remainder of
the fold. Fold the side *a, b, c,* to the line *a, e,*

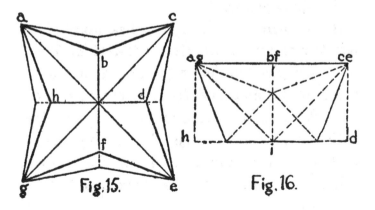

Fig. 15.   Fig. 16.

and sharpen the line from *a* to *b* only. Repeat this with the remaining three corners, and you will then find that you have a dish-shaped, four-cornered star, as in Fig. 15, the

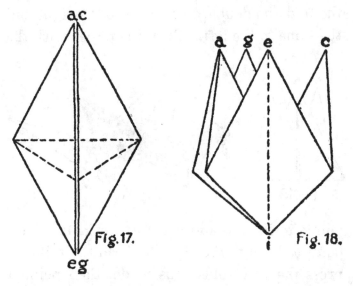

Fig. 17.   Fig. 18.

heavy lines showing the edge of the paper. Fold this star upward on the line *h, d,* with the sides doubled inward and you will have Fig. 16. Holding this with the thumb and fingers of both hands at the points marked *e* and *d,* bring the hands together, being sure that the points *b, f, h,* and *d* fold inward and down-

ward, and the result will be Fig. 17. After
this, fold the point *c* downward toward your
body and the point *a* downward in the opposite
direction, thus forming Fig. 18, and then open
the fold and double downward to the right and
the same to the left. Turn the paper with the

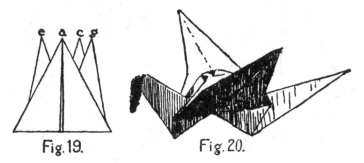

Fig. 19.   Fig. 20.

points to the top and you form Fig. 19. Pull
point *g* down to the right to form the tail and
press the new folds thus made, then point *e*
down to the left not quite so far, forming the
neck. To make the head, open the fold at *e*
and bend the head at right angles to the neck;
by pressing the folds together again the head
will take just the proper angle, as shown in
Fig. 20. Crush down the sharp point between
the wings *a* and *c,* and blow in the little hole

below the wings, which will inflate the body. The wings should be bent outward a little as shown. By holding the bird with the thumb and finger at the point marked *o*, and pulling the tail with the other hand, the wings can be made to flap.

THE BULLFROG

ANOTHER favorite folding stunt of my Japanese friend was the paper bullfrog, which is constructed as follows: Take a square of rather stiff paper eight or nine inches in size. Fold from corner to corner in both directions, making the lines *a, e,* and *c, g,* very sharply, then turn the paper the other side up and fold from side to side both ways, thus establishing the lines *b, f* and *h, d.* These serve as guide lines. (See Fig. 21.)

Fold the paper on the line *h, d,* with the fold pointing upward, and, holding it at *h, d,* with the thumb and finger of each hand, bring the hands toward each other. The sides will then fold inward and the points outward, following the guide lines, and form a four-pointed star. When the points *b, h* are folded together on the left, and *d, f* on the right, you will have a square with *i* at the top and *a, c, e, g* at the bottom. Lay this square on the

table with the point *i* away from the body,
lift up the point *f*, spread it open and flatten

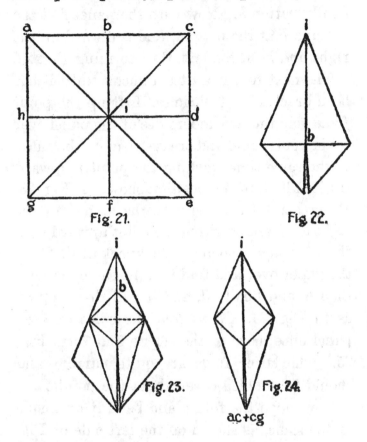

Fig. 21. Fig 22.

Fig. 23. Fig. 24.

ac+cg

it out with the line in the centre, forming new
folds on each side. Turn the paper over to

the right and flatten *d* in the same manner, then again to the right and flatten *b,* and finally flatten *h.* Now with the panel *f* at the top and *b* at the bottom, fold *d* inward on the right and *h* on the left, thus forming Fig. 22.

The next fold is a little difficult until it has been practised a few times. Lift up the point *f* and fold the two undersides of the panel over to the centre fold and crease them up the sides, at the same time working the point *f* upward till it falls into the position shown in Fig. 23. By creasing the sides with the fingers of the right hand and working the point upward with the left you will soon get the knack of it. Turn the paper over and fold *b* in the same manner, then *h,* and finally *d,* and it will then appear as in Fig. 24. Now, fold the sides of each panel once more to the centre and form Fig. 25. The latter folds are quite narrow and should be doubled carefully at the points.

Now, open the fold *a* and bend it up inside of the same, as shown on the left side of Fig. 26, and follow the same procedure with point *e* on the opposite side. Then fold outward

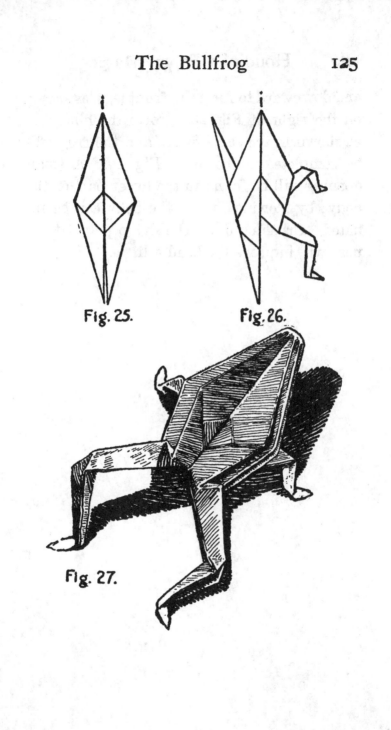

Fig. 25.

Fig. 26.

Fig. 27.

and downward to form the front legs, as shown
on the right of Fig. 26.   Form the hind legs
as shown in the same figure and the frog will
be complete, as shown in Fig. 27.   A small
opening will be found in the lower part of the
body; by blowing in this the body can be in-
flated.   Crushing down the sharp point at the
nose will improve the head a little.

PUZZLE BOX FOR SWEETS

THE best material for this box is rather heavy ledger paper, which should be cut in an exact square, the size depending on the size of the box required. If a twelve-inch sheet is used the box will be four and a quarter inches square.

In order to lay down the construction lines, first fold the sheet from corner to corner each way, then fold each corner down so that they all meet in the exact centre, as in Fig. 28. Flatten these lines with the back of the fingernail to serve as guides, as shown by the dotted lines in Fig. 29. Now open the sheet and fold down the four corners so that they will just reach the centre of the creases just made, as in Fig. 29, and flatten these lines also. Open the sheet again and fold the corner *a* to the crease *b*, as in Fig. 29. Flatten the fold, open out again and fold as shown in Fig. 29. Repeat this with the other three corners and

when the sheet is opened, if all the folds have
been flattened as directed, seven creases will

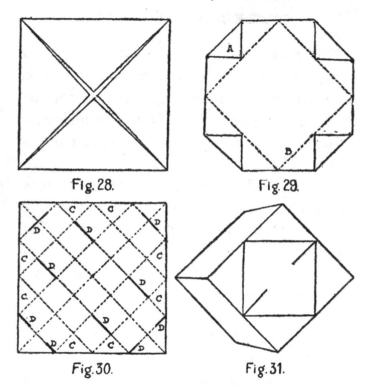

Fig. 28.

Fig. 29.

Fig. 30.

Fig. 31.

be found running diagonally across the sheet
in each direction, as shown by dotted lines in
Fig. 30.

Cut out the two centre triangles marked *c*

on all four sides and cut slits along the heavy lines marked *d*. You will then have at two of the corners pointed sections with a slit in the middle of each, and at the other corners like sections, but with the slits at the sides. Take one of the latter corners and bend the loose points—without creasing—and pass through the slit on the opposite corner. Smooth out bends and join the other corners in the same way, being careful that the loose squares fold inside the box, which will now appear as in Fig. 31, with the top securely fastened. To open the box, release the outer flap only, thus opening the sides.

WHY the name "Trouble Wit" should have been given to this form of paper folding is quite beyond my comprehension, for the manipulation is simple and easily acquired. The only thing about it that would trouble the wits is the original folding of the paper, as the successful production of the figures depends on careful and accurate folding and the selection of a suitable material. All this may be avoided, however, as all dealers in magical supplies carry the made-up article in stock and the price is nominal.

Trouble Wit is of very ancient origin and the fact that it is still in use proves its worth as a means of entertainment. Monsieur Trewey presented it throughout Europe and America under the name of "Papier Multiforme"; later Ellis Stanyon and others continued its popularity in London, and the late Adrian Plate made it a prominent feature of his program here.

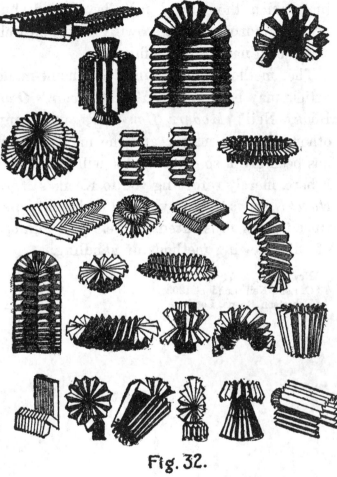

Fig. 32.

Fig. 32 shows a few of the favorite forms into which the "fan" may be shaped, but every performer has his own routine, as well as his own name for the figures.

The method of making the home-made article may be found in *The Magician's Own Book*,[1] Neil's *Modern Conjuror*,[2] and many other books on magic, and the manipulation has been given so often that I will not repeat it here, merely referring you to Keene's *More Novel Notions*,[3] where you will find eighty distinct figures illustrated, as well as a number of cuts showing methods of handling.

[1] New York, 1857.
[2] C. Lang Neil, London, 1903.
[3] Robertson Keene, London.

THE CHAPEAU

We have all had the experience of having some militant youngster bring us a newspaper with the request, "Make me a sojer hat." If we can produce something a little above the

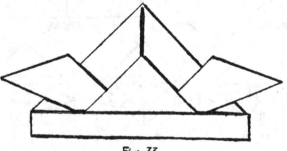

Fig. 33.

ordinary in that line we are sure to create a lasting impression of our greatness on that young mind.

The old-fashioned paper hat was a rather crude affair, but the Japanese, although this sort of headgear is entirely unknown in their country, have beaten us at our own game by producing a chapeau with two cockades, as shown in Fig. 33.

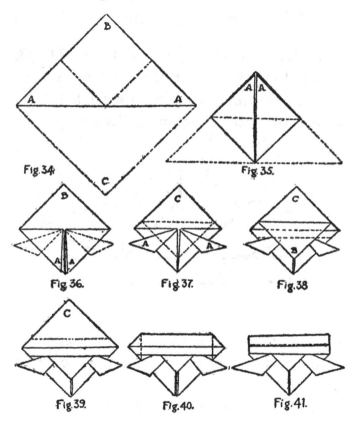

Fig. 34.

Fig. 35.

Fig 36.

Fig 37.

Fig. 38

Fig. 39.

Fig. 40.

Fig. 41.

To make this hat, take a piece of paper about eighteen inches square and fold from corner to corner, as in Fig. 34, and on the dotted lines, thus forming a square, as shown by the solid lines in Fig. 35. You will then have the points *a a* at the top, underneath them the corner *b,* and under that the corner *c.* Fold the points *a a* downward and form Fig. 36 and then fold the same points upward, as shown by the dotted lines, and form the two cockades shown in Fig. 37. Now fold the corner *b* downward on the dotted cross line to form Fig. 38 and make the narrow fold across the centre to bind the folds in place.

Next fold the corner *c backward* on the dotted line shown in Fig. 39, and the points backward as in Fig. 40; then make the narrow fold backward on the dotted line shown in Fig. 41, and the hat will be complete.

An added touch may be given by making a paper plume and tucking it into the upright fold.

THIS is a clever little conceit and a coin purse of this design made in leather, or imitation leather, might be found quite useful. The method of making it, while somewhat difficult

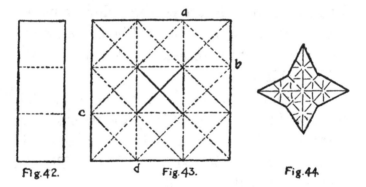

Fig. 42.   Fig. 43.   Fig. 44

to explain, is by no means hard to accomplish when it is once understood.

Cut a stiff piece of paper exactly square, fold from corner to corner in each direction and flatten the folds with the fingernail. Then fold in three equal parts (see Fig. 42), in the shape of an accordion, in each direction, as shown by the dotted lines *a, b, c,* and *d,* in Fig.

43, and flatten the folds. Open the paper and the folds will appear as in Fig. 43.

Now, pinch *a* and *b* together with the thumb and finger of the right hand, and *c* and *d* in like manner with the left, with the folds pointing downward, and bring the hands together.

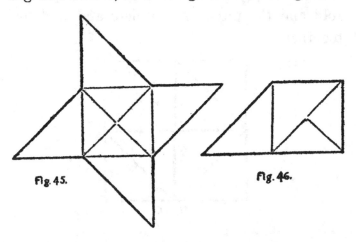

Fig. 45.   Fig. 46.

This will cause the opposite corners to shape themselves like the ones you hold, thus forming a sort of four-pointed star with the centre pointing downward. (See Fig. 44.) Next, twist the point held in the right hand away from your body and that in the left toward you, allowing the lines to place themselves, and

they will fall into the shape shown in Fig. 45.
Then, fold the lower point upward, the right-
hand point to the left and the top one downward, which brings the purse into the form
shown in Fig. 46.   Fold the left-hand point
toward the right and tuck it under the opposite
fold and the purse is complete and fastened
together.

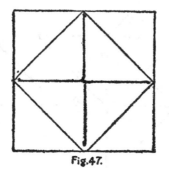

Fig. 47.

THIS is really a combination of six of the paper purses described on page 136. The centre

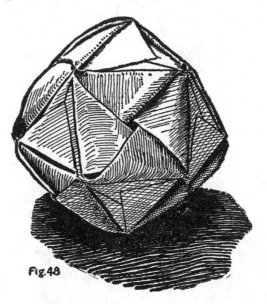

Fig. 48

cross lines in Fig. 43, which are shown by the solid lines, are cut and bent outward (see Fig. 47), and the loose flaps thus formed are pasted together in the manner shown in Fig. 48, thus forming a handsome hexagonal box, any one of the six sides of which can be easily opened and closed.

PART THREE
PAPER TEARING

POSSIBLY the late Monsieur Trewey was not
the first to use the paper rings on the stage,
but that genial performer made so much out
of this little trick that I think I may be for-
given for naming it after him.

In appearance the apparatus consists of
three bands or rings of newspaper, all exactly
alike, and a pair of scissors. As a matter of
fact, however, the rings are not "exactly"
alike, as will be shown.

The performer takes the first ring and cuts
it completely around the centre, as shown in
the dotted line in *a*, Fig. 49, the natural result
being two rings of the same diameter. But
when the second ring is cut in precisely the
same manner, instead of two rings a single
ring of double the diameter is produced (see
b, in Fig. 49). By repeating the operation

with the third band two rings, one linked within the other, result (see *c* in Fig. 49).

The secret lies in the preparation of the

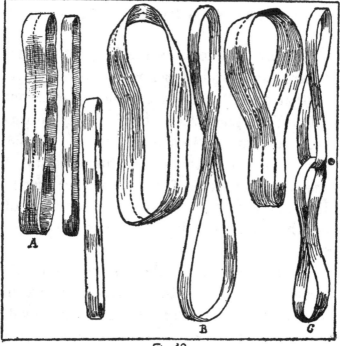

Fig 49

bands, which should be of newspaper cut in strips two inches wide and four or five feet long. The ends of the first strip are pasted together to form a ring, as shown in the illustration. The ends of the second strip are pasted in the same way except that this strip is given a single twist before the ends are joined. The same procedure is followed with the third, except that in this case a double twist is given. A glance at the illustration will make this perfectly plain. After this preparation the trick does itself.*

A very close observer might notice the twists in the second and third rings while none appears in the first. To guard against this I always give the first ring a twist *after it is joined,* which gives it the same appearance as the others.

If you desire to hurry the trick a little, lay the ring flat and cut the double thickness till within six or eight inches of the end, then drop one thickness and finish on the single paper. The latter move is not necessary with the first band, but it should be done, so that the cutting may always appear the same.

The paper may be torn instead of cut, if you so desire, and if it is introduced in a paper-tearing act this is much the better way.

When colored linen is used, this trick can be performed with greater certainty and effect.

No paper-tearing act is really complete without Jacob's Ladder. This is either torn from newspaper or, more effectively, as some consider, from several sheets of plain paper of different colors. There are two or three dif-

Fig. 50.   Fig. 51.

ferent ways of making the ladder, but the best in my opinion is as follows.

Use sheets of ordinary newspaper—the size is usually 22 by 36 inches—and fold a hem about one-half inch wide on the short side of the first sheet; roll *loosely* into a tube, leaving an open core of about an inch and a half. When this is six or eight inches from the end, insert another sheet and continue to roll, being careful not to make the roll too tight. The length of the ladder will depend on the number of sheets used and a trial will prove how many sheets you are able to tear. When the roll is complete, slip a rubber band on each end to keep it from unrolling.

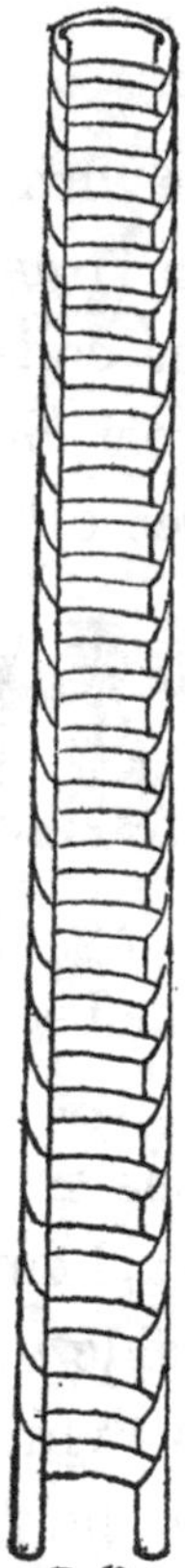

Flatten the roll, tear out the centre part, as shown in Fig. 50, and bend the ends downward, as in Fig. 51. The section torn away should be about two-thirds of the diameter of the roll.

To develop the ladder, hold the two ends in the left hand and with the right seize the hem and pull out the inner coils; then, by drawing out the spirals, first on one side and then on the other, the ladder can be projected upward six, eight, or ten feet, according to the number of sheets used. (See Fig. 52.)

Some performers begin with the sheets pasted together in a long strip and rolled up ready to tear, but I myself, on the

Fig. 52

theory that anything in the way of previous preparation weakens an effect, prefer the above method.

If huge sheets of paper are used, this trick is effective on a large stage.

Harry Moore, the English performer here with the Harry Lauder show, season 1921-22, tore a giant ladder, had a string lowered from the flies, and then leaned it against the back drop where he had a ladder camouflaged and apparently climbed up the paper ladder.

THE Trellis is in reality a variation of Jacob's Ladder, but the effect is quite dif-

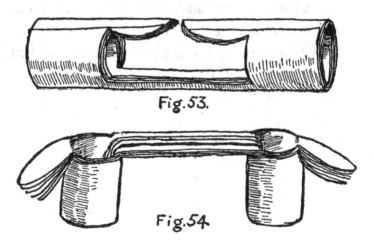

Fig. 53.

Fig. 54.

ferent, as will be seen by comparing the illustrations.

The roll is made in the same manner, but instead of tearing out the whole of the centre section two leaf-shaped ends are left, as shown

in Fig. 53. When the outer
ends are turned downward these
leaves are turned also and
pressed as flat as possible against
the roll (see Fig. 54.).

The Trellis is developed in
the same way as the ladder
by drawing out the inner folds
by means of the hem, the result being the handsome design
shown in Fig. 55.

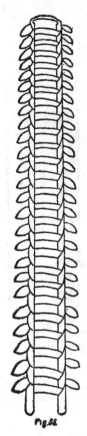

Fig. 55

THE Fir Tree should be torn from several strips of green paper and one strip of brown, the strips to be twelve inches wide and of any length. These are rolled into a rather loose tube, exactly as for Jacob's Ladder, the green strips first and then the brown.

Fig 56.

Put a rubber around one end of the roll and flatten the other end so that the solid line, shown in Fig. 56, will lie against one

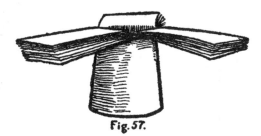

Fig. 57.

of the points indicated by the dotted lines. Tear both together straight down to a point a

little below the centre of the roll.
Then make the tear shown by the
other dotted line and fold the sections downward, as in Fig. 57.
Pull out the centre coils and the
tree shown in Fig. 58 will result,
its height depending on the number of strips used.

If the brown sections are torn
off before the tree is developed,
the result will be a green tree with
a brown trunk.

A good combination may be introduced by placing the tree in a
pot of earth and then remarking
that a ladder is necessary in order
to reach the top of the tree. Then
proceed to tear the Jacob's Ladder.

For stage work I would advise
using large sheets of paper, pasted
together.

Fig. 58

THE DANCING SKELETONS

ANOTHER favorite paper-tearing feat of that clever entertainer, Adrian Plate,[1] was the Dancing Skeletons. These gaunt gentlemen as they appear in Fig. 61 have a rather gruesome aspect, but when they are made to dance by shaking they are really very ludicrous. As someone remarked when Mr. Plate presented them before the Society of American Magicians, "They are ghastly funny."

Very few entertainers have made use of the skeletons, probably because it has not been realized how easily they can be produced nor how effective they can be made. My friend John W. Sargent, however, had the knack of tearing them, and the group here shown was torn by him and given to me, together with the details of the effect as he presents it.

The best material for this effect is the closely printed pages of a newspaper. I prefer the pages devoted to classified advertisements,

[1] Adrian Plate died February 24, 1919.

as they give to perfection, at a little distance, the whitish-gray color of the skeleton.

Take the double page of an ordinary daily, which is thirty-six inches wide when spread open, and lay it on a table with the inside of the sheet uppermost. This is done so that the middle fold will retain its original crease.

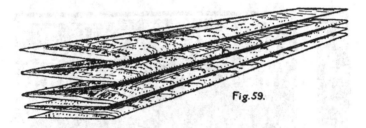

Fig. 59.

Now fold the edge nearest you to touch the crease in the centre and flatten the fold with the back of the thumb-nail. Fold the margin back even with the first fold, which will give a plait four and a half inches wide. Then turn the paper over and make another fold of the same size, and so on till the whole sheet is folded like an accordion. If the folds are carefully made the last margin will just reach to the edge. (See Fig. 59.) Next, tear out the portions appearing as black in Fig. 60, beginning at the edge showing the margin, so that the middle of the figure will come on the folds. Otherwise you will have two half-skeletons as "end-men."

To tear the eye-sockets, first fold across the skull horizontally at a point midway between

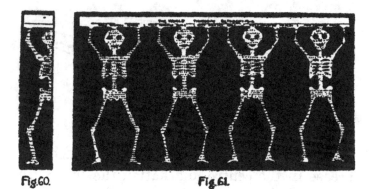

Fig. 60.   Fig. 61.

the mouth and the top of the head, and tear out a half-round piece. Be sure to get this large enough and also be sure to tear all the way through, so that the eyes will be the same size in all the figures. The ribs are torn in the same way and the same caution should be observed.

Unfold the skeletons one at a time and run the thumb-nail down the folds with the fore-finger at the back, thus "ironing out" the crease so that the figures will appear flat. (See Fig. 61.) Hold by the extreme upper corners and shake them gently, when they will per-form a very funny dance, which never fails to get a laugh and a round of applause.

PRESENTATION OF THE SKELETONS

The best method of presenting the skeletons is to start the tearing at the feet and tear out the fig're upside down. By this means the audience is kept in ignorance till the very end, while if the skull is made first they know what is coming and the interest is liable to flag some-what. It is an excellent idea to tell an ex-travagant ghost story while tearing and have your pianist introduce some spooky music.

The following bit of doggerel verse, by John W. Sargent,[1] makes a good finish:

[1] Sargent passed away September 24, 1920. He was my private secretary for three years; we had been friends for thirty years. He was well-known as a poet, and used this doggerel when he did the above trick.—H. H.

The King of Clubs, with thund'rous voice
  And frown as black as night,
Declares that war's his only choice—
  That might is always right.

The Plutocratic Diamond King
  Said, "Men can war no more
Unless our hoarded wealth we bring
  To liquidate the score."

The King of Hearts said, "War's a curse!
  For peace I'll still endeavor,
And if the worse comes to the worse
  I'll fight for peace forever."

The old, grave-digging King of Spades
  Said, "Stop this beastly row!
We'll all be like these grinning blades
  A few short years from now."

Fig 62.   Fig 63.

GRANDMA'S STRING OF DOLLS

A FAVORITE method of our grandmothers to
keep the little folks quiet was to cut or tear
out a string of dolls. This remains an equally
effective "weapon of amusement" to-day.
When entertaining children you will be surprised to find what a hit the dolls will make
with both boys and girls. (See Figs. 62 and
63.)

The directions given for the Dancing Skeletons apply equally well for the dolls. They
are often made of colored paper instead of
newspaper, and some performers make each
fold of a different color, strips of the proper
size being pasted together. By using thin

paper, eight or ten can easily be torn in a string, and there is always rivalry in the audience as to who shall receive them. By separating them into pairs they can be distributed, and sometimes a second string is demanded.

A story with the characters taken from Mother Goose makes a good accompaniment for tearing the dolls.

Fig.66.

THE DANCING GIRLS

These are really a sort of modernized version of Grandma's Dolls. They are made in the same way, except that the two legs in this case are not posed alike, so it will be neces-

Fig.64.

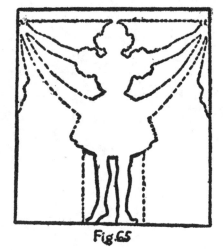

Fig.65

sary to tear them first as shown in Fig. 64 and then open one fold and tear the legs separately, as indicated in Fig. 65.

They can be made to dance in the same manner as the skeletons. (See Fig. 66.)

PAPER PICTURES

PICTURES torn from colored paper and displayed the same as the famous Rag Pictures can be made very effective, as shown in the frontispiece of this volume. The best paper for the purpose is the quality used in cheap posters. This can be had in all colors, in large sizes, is easily torn and is stiff enough to stay in place with very little pasting.

The different pieces may be partially torn out beforehand, that is, the more difficult ones may, so by tearing off a few corners the piece will be ready for use.

The lower part of the bridge, including the shadowy arches, can be torn in a few seconds. The gray and blue strips should be folded accordion shape in twelve folds and both torn together. Tear out one half of the arch on either edge of the fold and when opened six arches will appear. When applying the bridge to the picture, first put on the blue and over it the gray, slipping the latter far enough to the left to give the underarch effect. The upper part of the bridge is torn from the gray only, making two folds for each opening required. This is backed by a solid blue strip.

To construct the picture, first put on the sky colors, holding them in place with little dabs of glue from a small tube, which can be concealed in the hand, or with small pellets of magician's wax. This wax is made by softening beeswax with turpentine. After the sky is in place, put on the clouds, being careful to cover all the lines where the sky colors join. Then place the mountains, the river, and the green foreground. The outline of the river banks is made by tearing a dark and a light blue design of the same shape but the former should be a little the larger and should be mounted first, so that when the other is placed over it the dark margin will be shown. Finally place the details: house, fence, trees, etc.

This picture contains thirty-six pieces, eighteen each for the two performers, so it can be put together in a very short time if it has been properly rehearsed.

The board on which the pictures are made should be covered with several thicknesses of white paper, so that when a picture has been

Fig. 67.

shown the sheet can be torn away, leaving the surface ready for another. If the board is so constructed that it can be revolved, an added effect may be secured by making the picture upside down and swinging it into an upright position when finished.

The portrait (Fig. 67) is very simple and easily made. The best effect is obtained by making it on an orange background.

The entire black portion is in one piece. The sharp points should be cut nearly through beforehand, so that a little tearing will complete the outline. The outline for the face and neck can be sketched on a sheet of white paper with a faint pencil line and should be torn rather carefully. The positions of the eyes, nose and mouth can be indicated by pencil dots that are invisible at a few feet. The shadows on the neck and the gloved hand should be torn from newspaper evenly printed.

A fancy frame, torn from black paper and placed around the portrait, gives it the proper setting.

CIRCULAR DESIGNS

By all odds the most effective form of paper-tearing, either for drawing-room or stage, is that of circular, or, as they are sometimes called, wheel designs. Several well-known artists owe their popularity entirely to this form of entertainment, used in conjunction with songs or stories, the latter running a rather poor second.

Several writers have attempted to disclose the methods of the successful entertainers in this branch of artistry, but the designs submitted have in nearly every case proved to be but sorry travesties. This is probably owing to a lack of artistic ability on the part of the writer, together with a theory that any haphazard figure repeated many times in a circle produces an artistic design, as in the case of the kaleidoscope. While this theory is in a measure true, still no real success is possible in this art unless the composition and treatment are carefully thought out and thoroughly mastered.

The preparation for this effect is very simple. A number of large sheets of paper are folded beforehand in one of the modes shown in Fig. 68. I prefer the crossway fold for the first (see *A* in Fig. 68), rather than the

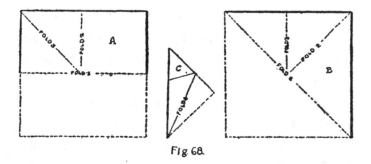

Fig. 68.

corner-to-corner fold as shown at *B* in the same figure; but in either case the result is the same in the fourth fold as shown at *C*. Sheets for special effects are folded differently, as will be shown further on.

In my own experience I have found the best paper for this work to be the quality used for large showbills, this being of a good white

which can be had in large sheets and is easy
to tear. The size of the sheets used will depend
on the size of the place of entertainment. For
the drawing-room a sheet three feet square
will give a good effect, while stage performers
often use sheets eight or nine feet square. The
manner of folding needs no explanation, as the
accompanying illustrations make it perfectly
plain. When folded four times as shown, a
figure torn on either edge will appear eight
times repeated in a circle when the paper is
unfolded. By making another fold the number of figures will be doubled, and still another
fold will produce thirty-two repetitions. Some
stage performers using very large sheets and
possessing very strong fingers, make even another fold, thereby producing sixty-four repli-
cas from a single tear. Thus if fifty figures are
torn the unfolded sheets will show thirty-two
hundred duplicates.

Considerable practice is necessary, as the
one great essential is rapidity, which can only
come through a thorough acquaintance with
the design and fingers trained to the work. A

singer who tears one design during his song may get away with it if the pattern is very handsome, but the chap who turns out a design for each verse, even if they are less complicated, is the one who gets the reëngagements. Always bear in mind the fact that a design may be artistic without being complicated. For example, a very good design may be made by tearing twenty-five figures in the two edges of the fold, and if an average speed of five seconds per figure is maintained the operation will be completed in two minutes and five seconds. In Fig. 72 only sixteen pieces are torn out and a very pretty pattern results.

For displaying the finished designs a black velvet curtain a little larger than the largest sheets used should be stretched rather tightly on a light frame, which may be made in sections for convenience in carrying, and the paper attached to it with pins. A gold braid around the edge of the velvet heightens the effect.

An added effect is produced by tearing the name of the theatre or the name of the performer in the margin of the design. (See Fig. 69.) Such artistic paper manipulators as the Brothers Coyne, who will be remembered by the older theatre-goers for their touching rendition of such songs as "A Letter from Dear

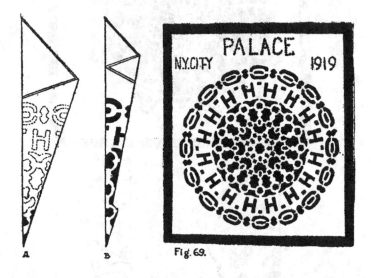

Fig. 69.

Old Ireland," made use of this effect, and it was always received with salvos of applause. I may also name another clever pair, Morton and Elliott, with whom I travelled in Europe several years ago, and for whose success I can personally vouch.

Fig. 70.

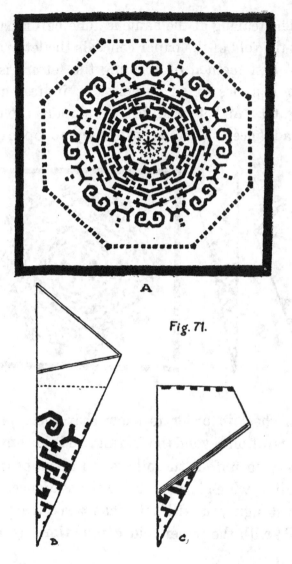

A

Fig. 71.

B   C,

The tearing of the name is done beforehand, but the fold of the paper conceals the lettering. The best method of forming the letters is to tear a series of small holes, as indicated in Fig. 69. As before stated, the paper is folded in advance, but it is customary to open the

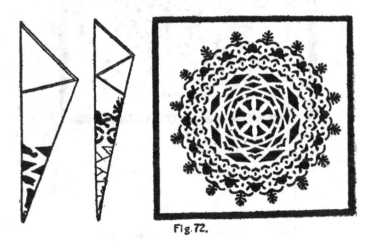

Fig. 72.

first sheet in order to show that there is no preparation beyond the folding, and it is unnecessary to unfold the others, as all appear to be alike, which is enough for the audience. In this design you will note that three tears are made with the paper folded four times (see *A* in Fig. 69), then another fold is made and the remaining figures torn. (See *B*.) This also shows a method of working initial letters into the design.

In the pattern shown in Fig. 70 also, a part is torn on four folds and a part on five. The cut is too small to show this design to advantage, but in a five or six-foot circle it is very effective.

Fig. 71 shows a Japanese model and the outer octagon of dentals is made by folding the top down on the dotted line in *B* and tearing out the squares shown in *C*.

THE FIVE-POINTED STAR

To make a five-pointed star with one stroke
of the scissors or a single tear, take a square
of paper about one-half larger than the size of
star desired and fold it in half as shown by *A*
in Fig. 73, the folded edge being at the bot-

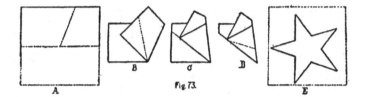

tom. Now fold the right-hand end toward the
left on a line running from the centre at the
bottom to a point one-third of the distance
from the right-hand corner at the top, as
shown by the dotted line on *A*, which will give
you *B*. Then fold from right to left on the
dotted line shown in *B*, thus forming *C*. After
this, fold the left-hand corner toward the right
underneath the other folds and the result will
be as in *D*. By cutting or tearing along the

dotted line there shown and unfolding the three-cornered section thus obtained, a perfect five-pointed star will be the result, as shown in *E*.

Care must be exercised in making the folds on exact lines, otherwise the points will be of unequal length and size. A little practice will enable you to make the folds and tear out a perfect star in from ten to twenty seconds.

MANY professional strong men have included in their programs the seemingly difficult feat of tearing one or two packs of playing cards in half, and then in quarters.

To tear two packs requires considerable strength of grip or very large hands, but to tear a single pack is extremely easy when the mode of procedure is known.

The general impression of those who see the thing done is that the pack is bevelled so that the tear starts on the edge of a single card, but it is quite impossible to tear a pack in that way. The pack should be squared up and held in an upright position in the left hand. Grasp the top firmly with the right hand, with all the fingers close together on the front and the heel of the hand on the back. Then seize the bottom with the left hand, using the same grip, but with the fingers on the back and the heel on the front, and bend the pack toward the right.

Twist the hands in opposite directions, turning the right *away* from the body, and you will be surprised to discover how easily the tear is made.

Slip a rubber band around one of the halves, toss it to your audience and tear the other half again in the same manner, putting a band on the quarters and offering them also for inspection.

The *bend* is very important, as this furnishes the fulcrum which replaces the main strength that would otherwise be necessary.

If a piece of tinplate the size of the cards and of the thickness formerly used for making the boxes for "Nabisco" biscuits, is placed in the middle of the pack, it can be torn with the cards with practically no more exertion. To an audience this has the appearance of a veritable feat of strength.

A telephone book of five hundred pages can be torn in two by a person of ordinary strength if one takes advantage of the bend.

PART FOUR
PAPER PUZZLES

AMONG paper puzzles the most ingenious are, without doubt, those formed along geometrical lines and generally designated by such names as "diagram," "dissected," or "cut-

Fig. 74.

up" puzzles. Of these the most ancient, and by all means the most remarkable, is that known as the Chinese Puzzle, which is said to have been invented by a renowned Chinese mathematician over 4000 years ago. It consists of a square of black cardboard cut into seven pieces, as shown in Fig. 74 and the number of combinations possible with them is as the sands of the sea.

The Chinese themselves were fond of forming such characters as are shown in Fig. 75, while the more modern "puzzle hound" prefers contriving architectural designs, like

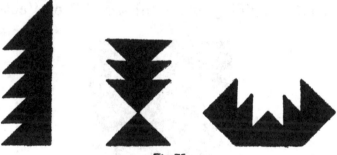

Fig. 75.

those in Fig. 76 or pictures, as in Fig. 77 and 78. That well-remembered puzzle king, Sam Lloyd, was particularly happy in constructing these pictures, and Figs. 77 and 78 are good examples of his art.

In 1902, at Eastbourne, England, I picked up a hand-made book bearing the title: A New Chinese Puzzle, in which 292 different hand-drawn designs are recorded, the entire seven

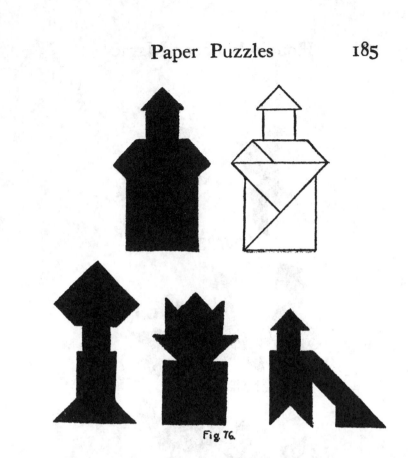

Fig 76.

pieces being used in each. On the fly-leaf of this book appears the name, A. Clowes, and the date, 1817. This is a manuscript copy and, I believe, the only one in existence.

LOVERS

THEIR FIRST

A BACK FENCE ARGUMENT   Fig. 77.

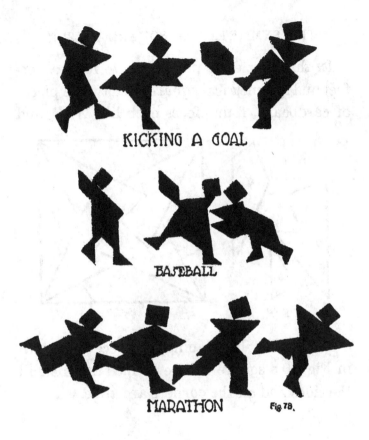

KICKING A GOAL

BASEBALL

MARATHON

Fig. 79.

THE SYMMETRICAL SQUARE PUZZLE

In this puzzle the problem is to form a perfect and symmetrical square with twelve pieces of cardboard, four pieces each like *A*, *B*, and

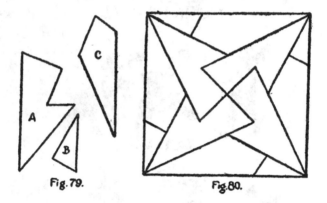

Fig. 79.   Fig. 80.

C in Fig. 79. By placing the pieces as shown in Fig. 80 a square will be formed in which all the sides and all the corners are alike.

THE problem here is to cut a square of cardboard in two pieces and with these two pieces
form the oblong figure *B,* or the irregular fig-

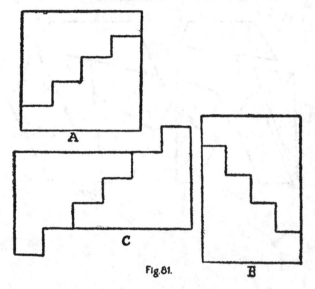

Fig. 81.

ure *C.* To accomplish this, cut the card as
shown by *A* in Fig. 81. By dropping the left
hand piece down one step *B* is obtained, while
dropping another step produces *C.*

THE HEXAGON PUZZLE

COMBINE the five pieces of cardboard shown in Fig. 82 so as to form a hexagon. Fig. 83 shows the proper arrangement.

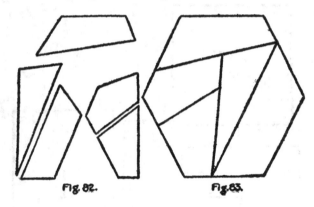

Fig. 82.　　　　Fig. 83.

THE OCTAGON PUZZLE

THE problem is to form an octagon with twelve pieces of cardboard, four of each of the shapes shown in Fig. 84. To reach this result, place the sections as seen in Fig. 85.

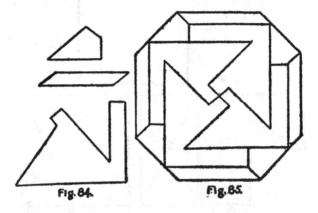

Fig. 84.   Fig. 85.

THE HOUSE AND ELL PUZZLE

A PIECE of cardboard cut to show the ground plan of a house and ell, as in Fig. 86, is to be cut into three sections by two straight cuts,

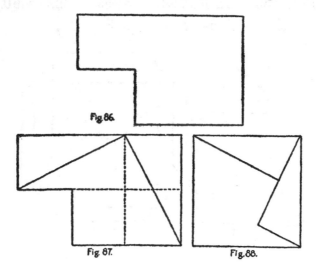

Fig. 86.

Fig. 87.

Fig. 88.

and the sections so joined as to form a perfect square. Cut along the *solid* lines in Fig. 87, the dotted lines being merely to establish the upper point, and place the three sections together as in Fig. 88.

THE CROSS AND CRESCENT

In this the problem is to divide a Greek cross into six sections, and with these sections to form a crescent. The cross is cut in curved

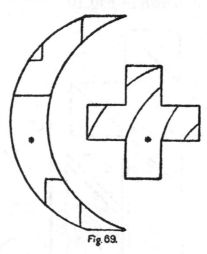

Fig. 69.

lines as shown in Fig. 89, and the crescent formed as there shown. The section marked with a star (*) has to be inverted and each outer end of the crescent is straight.

THE LATIN CROSS

FIRST METHOD.—To form a cross with five pieces of cardboard, one like *A*, one like *B*, and three like *C*, in Fig. 90. The manner of joining these is shown in Fig. 91.

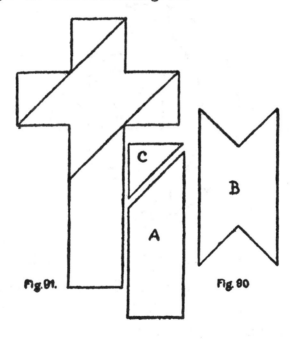

Fig. 91.

Fig. 90

Second Method.—In this five pieces are used also, three shaped like *A* and two like *B*, and the cross is formed by placing them as shown in Fig. 92.

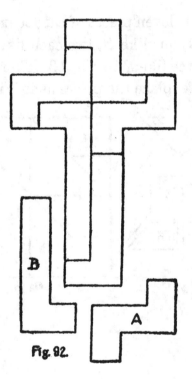

Fig. 92.

FOR this eleven pieces of cardboard are used,
one like *A*, one like *B*, two each like *C*, *D*, and
E, and three like *F* in Fig. 93. To form a perfect square, place the pieces as in Fig. 94.

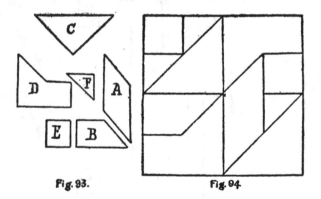

Fig. 93.   Fig. 94

THE RIGHT-ANGLE TRIANGLE

To form a perfect square from twenty pieces of cardboard cut in right-angle-triangular shape, *A* in Fig. 95. Place the sections in the positions shown in Fig. 96.

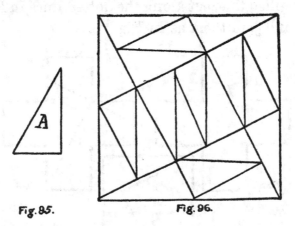

Fig. 95.

Fig. 96.

THE GREEK CROSS PUZZLE

A GREEK cross, Fig. 97, of paper or cardboard, may be so divided by two straight cuts that the resultant sections can be placed together and form a perfect square. To accomplish this, cut along the dotted lines in Fig. 98 and join them as in Fig. 99.

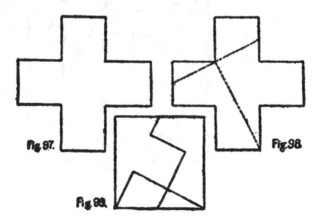

Fig. 97.   Fig. 98.

Fig. 99.

THE SQUARE DEAL PUZZLE

THE problem is to form a perfect square with five cardboard sections, one like *A,* two like *B* and two like *C,* in Fig. 100. The square is formed by placing the pieces as shown in Fig. 101.

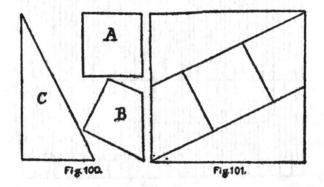

Fig. 100.   Fig. 101.

TO PASS THROUGH A CARD

THE problem is to cut a piece of cardboard in such a manner that a person can pass completely through it without tearing.

Fig. 102 gives you the idea complete.

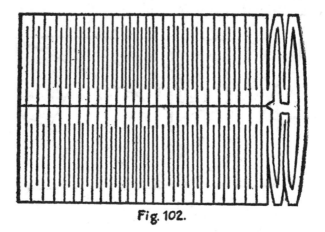

Fig. 102.

A piece of thin cardboard about four inches long and two and a half wide should be used. Fold it lengthwise in the centre and make straight cuts about an eighth of an inch apart from the fold nearly, but not quite, to the outer edges. Continue these cuts the length of the card as shown, then turn and cut from the edge, between the former cuts, almost to the fold. Then cut through the centre on the line of the fold, leaving the last section at each end uncut.

The card may then be drawn out into an endless chain, leaving an opening large enough for a man to pass it over his body.

A thin person could use a much smaller card.

To prepare for this puzzle, take an oblong
piece of Bristol board, fold it in the centre, and
cut out a liberty bell, as shown by *a,* in Fig.
103. The fold, being at the top, joins the two

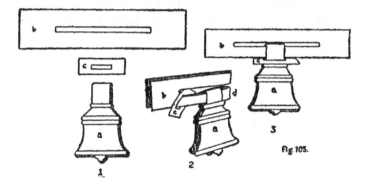

Fig. 103.

bells thus cut. Cut another piece with an opening in the centre, as shown by *b,* and another
like *c,* the opening in *c* being too small for the
bell to pass through. The relative sizes of the
several pieces are shown in the illustration.

The problem is to hang the bell on *b,* with *c*

around the top, as shown in 3, without bending the bell.

To accomplish this, bend *b* in the centre, as in 2, and pass *c* over the lower fold at *d;* then, hang the bell as shown and slip *c* back over the point *d* and down to the top of the bell. Now straighten out *b,* the fold in which should only be bent, not folded flat, so that when straightened it shows no indication of having been folded, and it will appear to be impossible to remove the bell without bending it.

THE CROSS CUT PUZZLE

Pass a card shaped like *A* in Fig. 104 to a friend and ask him to divide it by two straight cuts so that the resulting parts may be joined

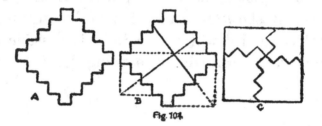

Fig. 104

together and form a perfect square. He will in all probability fail, and you can then show him how easy it is by cutting along the lines in *B*. The dotted lines show the points which determine the direction of the cuts.

THE THREE CROSSES

To form a Latin, Greek or Maltese cross, as shown in Fig. 105, by a single tear or cut, proceed as follows: For the Greek or Maltese form, a square piece of paper is used, as indicated

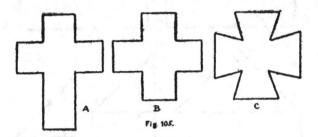

Fig. 105.

cated by the solid lines in *A*, Fig. 106, but for the Latin, the paper should be oblong, as shown by the broken lines at the bottom of the same diagram.

Fold the upper left-hand corner down on the dotted line in *A*, then the right-hand corner on the dotted line in *B*, and then on the centre line in *C*. If you have used the oblong paper you will now have the fold as in *D*, and by cutting along the dotted line in that diagram and

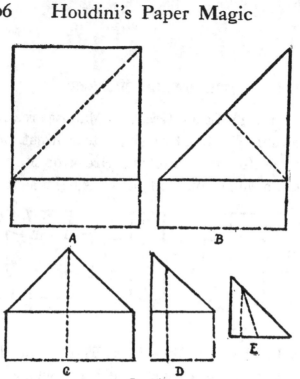

Fig. 106.

unfolding the paper, you will produce a perfect Latin cross.

But if you have used the square paper the third fold will give the diagram *E,* a cut along the left-hand dotted line of which will result in a Greek, and the right-hand in a Maltese cross.

A CATALOG OF SELECTED
DOVER BOOKS
IN ALL FIELDS OF INTEREST

A CATALOG OF SELECTED DOVER
BOOKS IN ALL FIELDS OF INTEREST

100 BEST-LOVED POEMS, Edited by Philip Smith. "The Passionate Shepherd to His Love," "Shall I compare thee to a summer's day?" "Death, be not proud," "The Raven," "The Road Not Taken," plus works by Blake, Wordsworth, Byron, Shelley, Keats, many others. Includes 13 selections from the Common Core State Standards Initiative. 112pp. 0-486-28553-7

ABC BOOK OF EARLY AMERICANA, Eric Sloane. Artist and historian Eric Sloane presents a wondrous A-to-Z collection of American innovations, including hex signs, ear trumpets, popcorn, and rocking chairs. Illustrated, hand-lettered pages feature brief captions explaining objects' origins and uses. 64pp. 0-486-49808-5

ADVENTURES OF HUCKLEBERRY FINN, Mark Twain. Join Huck and Jim as their boyhood adventures along the Mississippi River lead them into a world of excitement, danger, and self-discovery. Humorous narrative, lyrical descriptions of the Mississippi valley, and memorable characters. 224pp. 0-486-28061-6

ALICE STARMORE'S BOOK OF FAIR ISLE KNITTING, Alice Starmore. A noted designer from the region of Scotland's Fair Isle explores the history and techniques of this distinctive, stranded-color knitting style and provides copious illustrated instructions for 14 original knitwear designs. 208pp. 0-486-47218-3

ALICE'S ADVENTURES IN WONDERLAND, Lewis Carroll. Beloved classic about a little girl lost in a topsy-turvy land and her encounters with the White Rabbit, March Hare, Mad Hatter, Cheshire Cat, and other delightfully improbable characters. 42 illustrations by Sir John Tenniel. A selection of the Common Core State Standards Initiative. 96pp. 0-486-27543-4

THE ARTHUR RACKHAM TREASURY: 86 Full-Color Illustrations, Arthur Rackham. Selected and Edited by Jeff A. Menges. A stunning treasury of 86 full-page plates span the famed English artist's career, from *Rip Van Winkle* (1905) to masterworks such as *Undine,* *A Midsummer Night's Dream,* and *Wind in the Willows* (1939). 96pp. 0-486-44685-9

THE AWAKENING, Kate Chopin. First published in 1899, this controversial novel of a New Orleans wife's search for love outside a stifling marriage shocked readers. Today, it remains a first-rate narrative with superb characterization. New introductory note. 128pp. 0-486-27786-0

BASEBALL IS . . .: Defining the National Pastime, Edited by Paul Dickson. Wisecracking, philosophical, nostalgic, and entertaining, these hundreds of quips and observations by players, their wives, managers, authors, and others cover every aspect of our national pastime. It's a great any-occasion gift for fans! 256pp. 0-486-48209-X

THE CALL OF THE WILD, Jack London. A classic novel of adventure, drawn from London's own experiences as a Klondike adventurer, relating the story of a heroic dog caught in the brutal life of the Alaska Gold Rush. Note. 64pp. 0-486-26472-6

CANDIDE, Voltaire. Edited by Francois-Marie Arouet. One of the world's great satires since its first publication in 1759. Witty, caustic skewering of romance, science, philosophy, religion, government — nearly all human ideals and institutions. A selection of the Common Core State Standards Initiative. 112pp. 0-486-26689-3

THE CARTOON HISTORY OF TIME, Kate Charlesworth and John Gribbin. Cartoon characters explain cosmology, quantum physics, and other concepts covered by Stephen Hawking's *A Brief History of Time.* Humorous graphic novel–style treatment, perfect for young readers and curious folk of all ages. 64pp. 0-486-49097-1

THE CHERRY ORCHARD, Anton Chekhov. Classic of world drama concerns passing of semifeudal order in turn-of-the-century Russia, symbolized in the sale of the cherry orchard owned by Madame Ranevskaya. Showcases Chekhov's rich sensitivities as an observer of human nature. 64pp. 0-486-26682-6

A CHRISTMAS CAROL, Charles Dickens. This engrossing tale relates Ebenezer Scrooge's ghostly journeys through Christmases past, present, and future and his ultimate transformation from a harsh and grasping old miser to a charitable and compassionate human being. 80pp. 0-486-26865-9

CRIME AND PUNISHMENT, Fyodor Dostoyevsky. Translated by Constance Garnett. Supreme masterpiece tells the story of Raskolnikov, a student tormented by his own thoughts after he murders an old woman. Overwhelmed by guilt and terror, he confesses and goes to prison. A selection of the Common Core State Standards Initiative. 448pp. 0-486-41587-2

CYRANO DE BERGERAC, Edmond Rostand. A quarrelsome, hot-tempered, and unattractive swordsman falls hopelessly in love with a beautiful woman and woos her for a handsome but slow-witted suitor. A witty and eloquent drama. 144pp. 0-486-41119-2

A DOLL'S HOUSE, Henrik Ibsen. Ibsen's best-known play displays his genius for realistic prose drama. An expression of women's rights, the play climaxes when the central character, Nora, rejects a smothering marriage and life in "a doll's house." A selection of the Common Core State Standards Initiative. 80pp. 0-486-27062-9

DOOMED SHIPS: Great Ocean Liner Disasters, William H. Miller, Jr. Nearly 200 photographs, many from private collections, highlight tales of some of the vessels whose pleasure cruises ended in catastrophe: the *Morro Castle, Normandie, Andrea Doria, Europa,* and many others. 128pp. 0-486-45366-9

DUBLINERS, James Joyce. A fine and accessible introduction to the work of one of the 20th century's most influential writers, this collection features 15 tales, including a masterpiece of the short-story genre, "The Dead." 160pp. 0-486-26870-5

THE EARLY SCIENCE FICTION OF PHILIP K. DICK, Philip K. Dick. This anthology presents short stories and novellas that originally appeared in pulp magazines in the early 1950s, including "The Variable Man," "Second Variety," "Beyond the Door," "The Defenders," and more. 272pp. 0-486-49733-X

THE EARLY SHORT STORIES OF F. SCOTT FITZGERALD, F. Scott Fitzgerald. These tales offer insights into many themes, characters, and techniques that emerged in Fitzgerald's later works. Selections include "The Curious Case of Benjamin Button," "Babes in the Woods," and a dozen others. 256pp. 0-486-79465-2

ETHAN FROME, Edith Wharton. Classic story of wasted lives, set against a bleak New England background. Superbly delineated characters in a hauntingly grim tale of thwarted love. Considered by many to be Wharton's masterpiece. 96pp. 0-486-26690-7

FLATLAND: A Romance of Many Dimensions, Edwin A. Abbott. Classic of science (and mathematical) fiction — charmingly illustrated by the author — describes the adventures of A. Square, a resident of Flatland, in Spaceland (three dimensions), Lineland (one dimension), and Pointland (no dimensions). 96pp. 0-486-27263-X

FRANKENSTEIN, Mary Shelley. The story of Victor Frankenstein's monstrous creation and the havoc it caused has enthralled generations of readers and inspired countless writers of horror and suspense. With the author's own 1831 introduction. 176pp. 0-486-28211-2

THE GARGOYLE BOOK: 572 Examples from Gothic Architecture, Lester Burbank Bridaham. Dispelling the conventional wisdom that French Gothic architectural flourishes were born of despair or gloom, Bridaham reveals the whimsical nature of these creations and the ingenious artisans who made them. 572 illustrations. 224pp. 0-486-44754-5

THE GIFT OF THE MAGI AND OTHER SHORT STORIES, O. Henry. Sixteen captivating stories by one of America's most popular storytellers. Included are such classics as "The Gift of the Magi," "The Last Leaf," and "The Ransom of Red Chief." Publisher's Note. A selection of the Common Core State Standards Initiative. 96pp. 0-486-27061-0

THE GOETHE TREASURY: Selected Prose and Poetry, Johann Wolfgang von Goethe. Edited, Selected, and with an Introduction by Thomas Mann. In addition to his lyric poetry, Goethe wrote travel sketches, autobiographical studies, essays, letters, and proverbs in rhyme and prose. This collection presents outstanding examples from each genre. 368pp. 0-486-44780-4

GREAT ILLUSTRATIONS BY N. C. WYETH, N. C. Wyeth. Edited and with an Introduction by Jeff A. Menges. This full-color collection focuses on the artist's early and most popular illustrations, featuring more than 100 images from *The Mysterious Stranger, Robin Hood, Robinson Crusoe, The Boy's King Arthur,* and other classics. 128pp. 0-486-47295-7

HAMLET, William Shakespeare. The quintessential Shakespearean tragedy, whose highly charged confrontations and anguished soliloquies probe depths of human feeling rarely sounded in any art. Reprinted from an authoritative British edition complete with illuminating footnotes. A selection of the Common Core State Standards Initiative. 128pp. 0-486-27278-8

THE HAUNTED HOUSE, Charles Dickens. A Yuletide gathering in an eerie country retreat provides the backdrop for Dickens and his friends — including Elizabeth Gaskell and Wilkie Collins — who take turns spinning supernatural yarns. 144pp. 0-486-46309-5

HEART OF DARKNESS, Joseph Conrad. Dark allegory of a journey up the Congo River and the narrator's encounter with the mysterious Mr. Kurtz. Masterly blend of adventure, character study, psychological penetration. For many, Conrad's finest, most enigmatic story. 80pp. 0-486-26464-5

THE HOUND OF THE BASKERVILLES, Sir Arthur Conan Doyle. A deadly curse in the form of a legendary ferocious beast continues to claim its victims from the Baskerville family until Holmes and Watson intervene. Often called the best detective story ever written. 128pp. 0-486-28214-7

THE HOUSE BEHIND THE CEDARS, Charles W. Chesnutt. Originally published in 1900, this groundbreaking novel by a distinguished African-American author recounts the drama of a brother and sister who "pass for white" during the dangerous days of Reconstruction. 208pp. 0-486-46144-0

HOW TO DRAW NEARLY EVERYTHING, Victor Perard. Beginners of all ages can learn to draw figures, faces, landscapes, trees, flowers, and animals of all kinds. Well-illustrated guide offers suggestions for pencil, pen, and brush techniques plus composition, shading, and perspective. 160pp. 0-486-49848-4

HOW TO MAKE SUPER POP-UPS, Joan Irvine. Illustrated by Linda Hendry. Super pop-ups extend the element of surprise with three-dimensional designs that slide, turn, spring, and snap. More than 30 patterns and 475 illustrations include cards, stage props, and school projects. 96pp. 0-486-46589-6

THE IMITATION OF CHRIST, Thomas à Kempis. Translated by Aloysius Croft and Harold Bolton. This religious classic has brought understanding and comfort to millions for centuries. Written in a candid and conversational style, the topics include liberation from worldly inclinations, preparation and consolations of prayer, and eucharistic communion. 160pp. 0-486-43185-1

THE IMPORTANCE OF BEING EARNEST, Oscar Wilde. Wilde's witty and buoyant comedy of manners, filled with some of literature's most famous epigrams, reprinted from an authoritative British edition. Considered Wilde's most perfect work. A selection of the Common Core State Standards Initiative. 64pp. 0-486-26478-5

JANE EYRE, Charlotte Brontë. Written in 1847, *Jane Eyre* tells the tale of an orphan girl's progress from the custody of cruel relatives to an oppressive boarding school and its culmination in a troubled career as a governess. A selection of the Common Core State Standards Initiative. 448pp. 0-486-42449-9

JUST WHAT THE DOCTOR DISORDERED: Early Writings and Cartoons of Dr. Seuss, Dr. Seuss. Edited and with an Introduction by Rick Marschall. The Doctor's visual hilarity, nonsense language, and offbeat sense of humor illuminate this compilation of items from his early career, created for periodicals such as *Judge, Life, College Humor,* and *Liberty.* 144pp. 0-486-49846-8

KING LEAR, William Shakespeare. Powerful tragedy of an aging king, betrayed by his daughters, robbed of his kingdom, descending into madness. Perhaps the bleakest of Shakespeare's tragic dramas, complete with explanatory footnotes. 144pp. 0-486-28058-6

THE LADY OR THE TIGER?: and Other Logic Puzzles, Raymond M. Smullyan. Created by a renowned puzzle master, these whimsically themed challenges involve paradoxes about probability, time, and change; metapuzzles; and self-referentiality. Nineteen chapters advance in difficulty from relatively simple to highly complex. 1982 edition. 240pp. 0-486-47027-X

LEAVES OF GRASS: The Original 1855 Edition, Walt Whitman. Whitman's immortal collection includes some of the greatest poems of modern times, including his masterpiece, "Song of Myself." Shattering standard conventions, it stands as an unabashed celebration of body and nature. 128pp. 0-486-45676-5

LES MISÉRABLES, Victor Hugo. Translated by Charles E. Wilbour. Abridged by James K. Robinson. A convict's heroic struggle for justice and redemption plays out against a fiery backdrop of the Napoleonic wars. This edition features the excellent original translation and a sensitive abridgment. 304pp. 0-486-45789-3

LIGHT FOR THE ARTIST, Ted Seth Jacobs. Intermediate and advanced art students receive a broad vocabulary of effects with this in-depth study of light. Diagrams and paintings illustrate applications of principles to figure, still life, and landscape paintings. 144pp. 0-486-49304-0

LILITH: A Romance, George MacDonald. In this novel by the father of fantasy literature, a man travels through time to meet Adam and Eve and to explore humanity's fall from grace and ultimate redemption. 240pp. 0-486-46818-6

LINE: An Art Study, Edmund J. Sullivan. Written by a noted artist and teacher, this well-illustrated guide introduces the basics of line drawing. Topics include third and fourth dimensions, formal perspective, shade and shadow, figure drawing, and other essentials. 208pp. 0-486-79484-9

THE LODGER, Marie Belloc Lowndes. Acclaimed by *The New York Times* as "one of the best suspense novels ever written," this novel recounts an English couple's doubts about their boarder, whom they suspect of being a serial killer. 240pp. 0-486-78809-1

MACBETH, William Shakespeare. A Scottish nobleman murders the king in order to succeed to the throne. Tortured by his conscience and fearful of discovery, he becomes tangled in a web of treachery and deceit that ultimately spells his doom. A selection of the Common Core State Standards Initiative. 96pp. 0-486-27802-6

MANHATTAN IN MAPS 1527–2014, Paul E. Cohen and Robert T. Augustyn. This handsome volume features 65 full-color maps charting Manhattan's development from the first Dutch settlement to the present. Each map is placed in context by an accompanying essay. 176pp. 0-486-77991-2

MEDEA, Euripides. One of the most powerful and enduring of Greek tragedies, masterfully portraying the fierce motives driving Medea's pursuit of vengeance for her husband's insult and betrayal. Authoritative Rex Warner translation. 64pp. 0-486-27548-5

THE METAMORPHOSIS AND OTHER STORIES, Franz Kafka. Excellent new English translations of title story (considered by many critics Kafka's most perfect work), plus "The Judgment," "In the Penal Colony," "A Country Doctor," and "A Report to an Academy." A selection of the Common Core State Standards Initiative. 96pp. 0-486-29030-1

METROPOLIS, Thea von Harbou. This Weimar-era novel of a futuristic society, written by the screenwriter for the iconic 1927 film, was hailed by noted science-fiction authority Forrest J. Ackerman as "a work of genius." 224pp. 0-486-79567-5

THE MYSTERIOUS MICKEY FINN, Elliot Paul. A multimillionaire's disappearance incites a maelstrom of kidnapping, murder, and a plot to restore the French monarchy. "One of the funniest books we've read in a long time." — *The New York Times.* 256pp. 0-486-24751-1

NARRATIVE OF THE LIFE OF FREDERICK DOUGLASS, Frederick Douglass. The impassioned abolitionist and eloquent orator provides graphic descriptions of his childhood and horrifying experiences as a slave as well as a harrowing record of his dramatic escape to the North and eventual freedom. A selection of the Common Core State Standards Initiative. 96pp. 0-486-28499-9

OBELISTS FLY HIGH, C. Daly King. Masterpiece of detective fiction portrays murder aboard a 1935 transcontinental flight. Combining an intricate plot and "locked room" scenario, the mystery was praised by *The New York Times* as "a very thrilling story." 288pp. 0-486-25036-9

THE ODYSSEY, Homer. Excellent prose translation of ancient epic recounts adventures of the homeward-bound Odysseus. Fantastic cast of gods, giants, cannibals, sirens, other supernatural creatures — true classic of Western literature. A selection of the Common Core State Standards Initiative. 256pp. 0-486-40654-7

OEDIPUS REX, Sophocles. Landmark of Western drama concerns the catastrophe that ensues when King Oedipus discovers he has inadvertently killed his father and married his mother. Masterly construction, dramatic irony. A selection of the Common Core State Standards Initiative. 64pp. 0-486-26877-2

OTHELLO, William Shakespeare. Towering tragedy tells the story of a Moorish general who earns the enmity of his ensign Iago when he passes him over for a promotion. Masterly portrait of an archvillain. Explanatory footnotes. 112pp. 0-486-29097-2

THE PICTURE OF DORIAN GRAY, Oscar Wilde. Celebrated novel involves a handsome young Londoner who sinks into a life of depravity. His body retains perfect youth and vigor while his recent portrait reflects the ravages of his crime and sensuality. 176pp. 0-486-27807-7

A PLACE CALLED PECULIAR: Stories About Unusual American Place-Names, Frank K. Gallant. From Smut Eye, Alabama, to Tie Siding, Wyoming, this pop-culture history offers a well-written and highly entertaining survey of America's most unusual place-names and their often-humorous origins. 256pp. 0-486-48360-6

PRIDE AND PREJUDICE, Jane Austen. One of the most universally loved and admired English novels, an effervescent tale of rural romance transformed by Jane Austen's art into a witty, shrewdly observed satire of English country life. A selection of the Common Core State Standards Initiative. 272pp. 0-486-28473-5

Browse over 10,000 books at www.doverpublications.com